Successful Meetings
In A Week

David Cotton

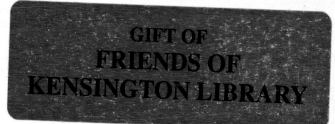

GIFT OF
FRIENDS OF
KENSINGTON LIBRARY

The Teach Yourself series has been trusted around the world
for over 60 years. This series of 'In A Week' business books is
designed to help people at all levels and around the world to
further their careers. Learn in a week, what the experts learn
in a lifetime.

David Cotton is an independent leadership and management trainer, with experience of working in four continents and more than 35 countries. His client portfolio reads like a 'Who's Who' of major organizations in local and national government and nearly every industry sector. He spent more than 20 years with two of the 'Big 4' professional service firms before setting up his own training consultancy. He has written 10 books, two of which won publishers' bestseller awards, scores of journal articles and a double award-winning e-learning package on electronic marketplaces. In that time, he has spent many thousands of hours in meetings and estimates that 75 per cent of that time was wasted. He has written this book to help you to spend your time more productively.

Acknowledgements

Thanks to Michael Whitwell and Christopher Barrat for sharing valuable ideas and insights. Thanks to Jane Cotton for support. Thanks to the thousands of people I've met across the meeting table for the huge fun those meetings provided.

Successful Meetings

David Cotton

www.inaweek.co.uk

Teach Yourself®

Hodder Education

338 Euston Road, London NW1 3BH.

Hodder Education is an Hachette UK company

First published in UK 2012 by Hodder Education

First published in US 2012 by The McGraw-Hill Companies, Inc.

www.hoddereducation.co.uk

Typeset by Cenveo Publisher Services.

Printed in Great Britain by CPI Group (UK) Ltd, Croydon, CR0 4YY.

Contents

Introduction

Business is all about conversations. Whether you are in manufacturing, a service industry, farming, a local or national government department, working as a sole trader or are the chief executive officer of a global organization, we all ultimately do business by talking to each other. We can hold our conversations one to one or in groups, in small, formal or informal gatherings, in major conferences or through social media. We cannot avoid meetings!

The online dictionary service, dictionary.com, defines a meeting as:

1 the act of coming together
2 an assembly or conference of persons for a specific purpose
3 the body of persons present at an assembly or conference
3 and, rather interestingly:
4 a hostile encounter; duel.

Whatever our reason for meeting others, a vast number of people feel that they are wasting time in meetings when they could more usefully be getting on with their work. Yet a well-managed, purposeful meeting can be highly motivating. This book will show you how to achieve that and will help you enormously in your professional career.

Whether you are participating or chairing, this book will help you to develop the skills you need to make meetings effective and get the most out of them.

It's divided into seven chapters, each of which deals with a different aspect of successful meetings. Read a chapter a day and by the end of the week you should feel a great deal more confident.

On our first day, Sunday, we'll look at why we hold meetings at all.

The key to successful meetings is preparation, and Monday is all about the things you need to do before a meeting to make it a success.

Have you ever attended a meeting in which some people remained silent throughout? Did you wonder afterwards why they were invited at all, when they contributed nothing? If you're a little nervous about speaking in front of others, you may miss the moment to have your say and could leave a meeting thinking, 'I wish I had just said what I was thinking!' Tuesday is all about participating in a meeting and having your say, regardless of the seniority of the others around the meeting table.

Increasingly it is becoming common to rotate the chairing of regular meetings and so, even if you're relatively junior at work, you may find yourself asked to assume the role of Chair. On Wednesday, you'll learn all about the duties, skills and responsibilities of a meeting Chair.

We tend to think of meetings as a group of people sitting around a table discussing matters of shared interest. There are many alternatives to the standard meeting, and on Thursday we'll explore some of them, from one-to-one meetings to online meetings, from audio conferences to large conference-style meetings.

It's not enough simply to hold a meeting and then go back to work as though the meeting never took place. On Friday, we'll look at what happens after a purposeful meeting – at follow-up activities for both the Chair and the participant.

Finally, on Saturday, we'll bring everything together in a story about two relatively junior colleagues who are asked to run a meeting for the first time. We'll see them learning from their mistakes and creating checklists to help them the next time they run a meeting. Is their meeting a success? You'll have to wait and see!

SUNDAY

Why meetings?

If all else fails, we can always have a meeting. Meetings have become the standard default means of exchanging information and sharing ideas at work, and often we do not consider the alternatives that could save us time and allow us to achieve more.

Today we're going to set the scene for the rest of our week. We'll look at why we hold meetings, whether formal or informal, and explore some of the best reasons for meeting with others. In each case we'll spend a little time looking at how those meetings can successfully achieve their aims. We'll look, too, at less useful reasons for holding a meeting.

We'll look at how much time we spend in meetings, and how much of this people feel is wasted time. We'll see how we can determine whether a meeting is the most appropriate channel for achieving a business objective or whether alternatives may be preferable.

What's a meeting?

In the ideal world, a meeting is a chance for people with shared or developing interests in a common theme to come together to further develop those interests. By the end of the meeting, something should have changed – participants may have agreed on something new, discovered something new or changed their thinking about something. Whatever the purpose of the meeting, it should result in some change, whether immediate or as a result of the meeting.

A meeting should:

- have a purpose
- bring together people with shared interest in achieving that purpose
- result in change.

A good meeting is action focused. It's not simply a talking shop, but a productive mechanism for making things happen. Just as the best production line streams out high-quality goods as efficiently and effectively as possible, so the best meeting generates focused actions as efficiently and effectively as possible.

> **Effectively – doing the right things**
> **Efficiently – doing things right**

A waste of time

It has been estimated that 11 million meetings take place in the USA every day[1] and that most professionals attend nearly 62 meetings per month.[1] Research suggests that more than 50 per cent of this meeting time is wasted time.[2]

If each meeting is just one hour long, this means that people are spending 31 hours (around four working days) every month in unproductive meetings.

Most people meeting regularly say they daydream (91 per cent), miss meetings (96 per cent) or miss parts of meetings (95 per cent). Many (73 per cent) say they bring other work to meetings and 39 per cent say they have fallen asleep during meetings.[3]

SUNDAY
MONDAY
TUESDAY
WEDNESDAY
THURSDAY
FRIDAY
SATURDAY

Whether or not it is reasonable to extrapolate these figures for other nations based on their relative population size, you can see that meetings have received a bad press over the years, and quite deservedly so.

Bad meetings lack purpose and focus and are badly chaired; the agenda is unclear or absent, dominant people use the meeting as a platform for their own political interests and others feel that they have no voice.

Meanwhile, everyone's *real* work piles up as the meeting grinds on inexorably to a stuttering finish. Does this sound familiar?

Reasons not to hold a meeting

Let's think about some good reasons not to hold a meeting (although we often do) and get these out of the way, so that we look positively at good reasons to meet and how those reasons can be translated into productive effort.

Actually, it doesn't matter on which day of the week the meeting is held. The regular monthly, weekly or (alarmingly) daily meeting suffers from the very reason it was initiated – its regularity. The first time a team decides to meet regularly, there is relative enthusiasm. People see the point. It's a chance to get together as a team, talk about things of mutual interest and share information which may be useful to others. It doesn't take long for meetings to turn stale and for people to start attending out of a sense of duty or fear of reprisals. People go over the same old ground, jokes are repeated and the same people use it as a platform for their own intentions whether or not these are relevant to the subject of the meeting.

> I once had a client that was a sales-driven organization obsessed by its weekly figures and reactive to any slight short-term change in its profitability. One of its sales teams held a regular Monday morning meeting. The team's manager told me that this was a motivational event, designed to kick-start the week on a high. He encouraged me to attend to see how it worked in practice.
>
> He began by announcing that Terry (name changed to protect the innocent) had exceeded his sales target by 4 per cent.
>
> 'What do we say to Terry?', he exclaimed.
> 'Hurrah!', they all shouted.
> 'Now Joan missed her target by 2.5 per cent. What do we say to Joan?'
> 'Boo!', they all cried.
> I later asked him what he thought he was doing.
> 'Motivating Joan', he said.

Regular meetings tend to reflect short-term thinking. For example, a sales team will meet once a week to discuss the sales figures of the previous week. The danger in focusing on the short term is that you miss longer term trends and read too much into glitches or exceptional situations. It's important, of course, to rectify immediate problems, but it's more important to assess how an organization is performing over a longer period.

The sole purpose of the 'blame fest' seems to be to point fingers at any hint of underperformance. If you think in the short term, you're more likely to find fault with individuals based on a single error or on a single week in which they appeared to underperform. The blame fest is a power play for the person who runs the meeting and is desperately embarrassing for participants, who may wonder 'Will it be my turn this time?' While teams often perform well for limited periods under pressure, they do not perform well out of fear, and blame fests simply make people frightened.

Perhaps controversially, meetings are not a great forum for information sharing. We have excellent electronic tools for just this. (E-mail is not one of them! When a person leaves, the vital information buried in their account disappears from sight.) Often, organizations hold meetings to share information because they think their employees do not read important e-mailed information. If a piece of information is relevant to someone's job and they either do not read it or do not act it on it, then that becomes a management issue rather than a reason to hold meetings.

It may be that e-mail is simply not the right medium for disseminating information. Equally, it may be that too much information is sent too often, written in language people do not understand, the e-mails are too long, the distribution list is too broad, the content isn't relevant or it's just plain boring...

One example of useful information-sharing software is Lotus Notes, which is designed to allow teams to share information using 'databases' which are really information-sharing or knowledge management repositories. In organizations where Notes is well used, teams are kept completely up to date on everything their members are doing. They do not need to meet to share this knowledge – they already have it, whether they are working in the same location or are geographically spread.

Reasons to hold a meeting

Let's explore some of the better reasons for holding a meeting. They are in no particular order, and it may be that within your organization you are aware of other good reasons. Make sure that they meet the three criteria that we set out a little earlier.

Here are two different scenarios:

1 A board of directors must decide whether to spend a large amount of money on something which may be risky for their business. If it works, it could result in a massive increase in profitability. Failure could mean financial disaster. The directors have always worked well together, buying into the company's

strategic vision and understanding how actions taken in one area of the business will affect work in the other areas.

2 The manager of a team working in a single location has been approached by a stationery company offering printer paper at lower cost and at a slightly lower quality.

Which of these decisions merits a formal meeting? One, both or neither? What criteria would you apply to determine whether it's appropriate to hold a meeting to make these decisions?

Here are some ideas:

1 Could the decision be taken by one person alone?
2 Do they have authority to make the decision?
3 What are the potential outcomes of the decision?
4 How many people do the outcomes affect?
5 If the wrong decision is made, what would happen to the decision-maker?
6 Is it morally acceptable for one person to make the decision?
7 Is it commercially wise for one person to make the decision?
8 Does any single person have the expertise to make the decision alone?

On that basis, it should be clear that in the first scenario, a meeting of all the directors is necessary. In the second scenario, the manager should be able to make the decision alone. We can take democracy at work too far!

Collaborative decision-making is a useful purpose for a meeting, where it is right and proper that the decision should fall to more than one person. Enlisting a wider group of people to make decisions brings its own problems, which we'll see when we look at chairing skills. It also brings different perspectives, which can be useful for seeing an argument from more than one side.

Your long-established team is about to undertake a new project. Members know each other very well and have worked on many projects in the past. The team leader has e-mailed details of the project to you all and has assigned project roles and responsibilities. You are happy to start on the new project but something doesn't feel right. What's missing?

At the start of any new project, whether involving a new or established team, it's useful to meet and talk through how you will work together. Team members may spot issues which have not been addressed by the team leader, may want to ask questions about project specifics and may even feel that the first meeting is the formal start to the project.

At the end of a project, it's great practice to hold a debrief meeting.

A bad debrief ends up as a blame fest, in which people have to account for mistakes they have made along the way.

A good debrief is all about what is called *double-loop learning*. Imagine you go to the doctor because you have a rash on your hand. A bad doctor gives you some cream and tells you to apply it three times a day and the rash will disappear. A good doctor examines you more thoroughly to understand the underlying causes of the rash. *Single-loop learning* addresses symptoms, sticking a plaster over the problem in the hope that it won't recur. Double-loop learning finds the underlying cause of a problem and changes systems or processes so that the problem cannot recur.

A good project debrief will:

1 Blamelessly discover the underlying causes of problems which occurred during the project and change working practices so that the problems cannot recur in future projects.
2 Discover the things which worked well and determine whether they can be built into new 'best practices'.

Ten people are brought together to form a new team. Some have met before, some are complete strangers to each other and some know others only by name or by reputation. It's useful for any new team to meet and get to know something about each other. Give them time to chat, mix socially, talk one to one and discover something about each other, both professionally and personally.

New teams are said[4] to go through a number of stages – 'forming', 'norming' and 'storming' – before they reach the intended goal of 'performing'.

At the forming stage, they are polite and a little formal, evaluating and trying to understand each other. At the storming stage, politeness is replaced by some jostling for position, and team members become more assertive in carving out the most appropriate role for themselves. At the norming stage, people have begun to find their feet, roles and responsibilities are clearer and ways of working have been established.

Because the team has been set up to perform at its best, it's important to get through these early stages as quickly as possible. One way to speed up the process is to get the team members together as early as possible so that they can assess each other face to face.

> As a consultant to many organizations, I am often asked to give opinions. This is a reasonable request – I can often bring a fresh perspective based on experience of working with many other organizations in the same or different sectors.
>
> Sometimes, however, I am asked to ratify silly decisions made by senior people who have played the dangerous business game of 'ready, fire, aim!' They have made a decision and probably realized it was inappropriate but, having announced it to their staff, lack the courage or humility to admit that there may be a better option and bring me in to agree to it so they can tell their staff that an outside consultant told them it was the right decision...
>
> If you meet others to seek their expertise, use their views and experience to help shape your own decisions rather than as a validation of a misguided decision which you've already put into operation. (And beware of the consultants who *will* ratify your thinking because they want the fee.)

Traditionally, teams worked in the same place. Globalization and expansion of organizations, a need to serve people locally and a desire to cut costs have led to increasing numbers of people working from home, only occasionally visiting an office, and geographically scattered teams with few opportunities to meet up. This increase in 'virtual teams' can result in people feeling isolated and dissociated from both each other and the organization. It is important for a new virtual team to meet each other face to face. Just as for the new team working in the same physical space, members will go through the forming, storming and norming stages, but physical separation of the virtual team makes this extremely difficult.

Bring them together at the outset and, whenever possible, arrange other opportunities for them to meet. As we'll see on Thursday, there are ways to bring them together virtually, too.

We negotiate constantly at work. Each of us wants something a little different (or completely different) and we negotiate to get the possible deal. It is far easier to negotiate face to face because it allows us to see, in the moment, others' reactions to our ideas. Globalized markets mean that often we have to negotiate by telephone, video conference or other virtual means. Whatever the chosen medium, the meeting is the basis for our negotiations.

It's unlikely that you know the answer to every problem which faces you at work. Luckily, if your network is good, you'll know someone with more expertise than you. Meet them and draw on their experience. Try not to influence their decision as you state your problem – present it objectively, as factually and as clearly as possible. The most useful experts ask good, often penetrating, questions before offering advice. Often they will not tell you the course of action to take, but help you to understand the consequences of the options available to you so you can make an informed judgement.

A team leader or manager has agonized over a solution to a problem and has determined a possible action. They now ask others to come and help them to work through their solution to identify its strengths and weaknesses.

Summary

When you invite others to a meeting you are taking some of their most valuable resource – time. Time is short and time is money. You cannot afford the luxury of time in a meeting if your time would be better spent elsewhere.

Equally, you cannot afford to work in isolation from others because the organization isn't all about *you*.

If you are in a position to decide on the best way to tackle a business issue, consider the three criteria for a meeting: purpose, bringing people together who have shared interests in achieving that purpose and bringing about change. If others decide on your behalf that a meeting is the best channel to resolve an issue and you can't see how a meeting would achieve that objective, then have the courage to question its validity.

At every level in an organization, it's worth considering two things: stewardship and legacy. Nobody stays in an organization forever, and most organizations are unlikely to last forever! You are the temporary steward of an organization. If you continue to adopt practices which you know are inappropriate

SUNDAY

MONDAY

TUESDAY

WEDNESDAY

THURSDAY

FRIDAY

SATURDAY

or inadequate, then you are perpetuating and institutionalizing mediocrity and thus your legacy to others will be poor.

Picture this: you have a new member in your team, a fresh-faced youth who asks in all innocence 'What's the purpose of the Monday morning meeting?' If your truthful answer is 'We've always had a Monday morning meeting' and you can think of no more positive reasons for it, then shame on you! It's terrible stewardship and a woeful legacy...

Fact-check (answers at the back)

1. One of the primary purposes of meetings is:
   - a) To help people to feel important in their work ❑
   - b) To result in change ❑
   - c) To motivate people whose morale is low ❑
   - d) To help people to network more widely in the organization ❑

2. A meeting is the best way to:
   - a) Share information ❑
   - b) Provide a platform for senior people to air their views ❑
   - c) Kick-start a virtual team ❑
   - d) Manage an organization ❑

3. Research suggests that the percentage of meeting time which people feel is wasted is:
   - a) 50 per cent ❑
   - b) 20 per cent ❑
   - c) 30 per cent ❑
   - d) 70 per cent ❑

4. Which of the following is typically not a good basis for a meeting?
   - a) Collaborative decision-making ❑
   - b) The regular weekly meeting ❑
   - c) Project initiation ❑
   - d) Seeking opinions and expertise ❑

5. Which of the following is a potential benefit of a project debrief meeting?
   - a) Zero-loop learning ❑
   - b) Single-loop learning ❑
   - c) Double-loop learning ❑
   - d) Triple-loop learning ❑

6. At the 'storming' stage in a team's evolution, team members:
   - a) Ignore each other in favour of their own political ends ❑
   - b) Display anger and become aggressive ❑
   - c) Complain about colleagues behind their backs ❑
   - d) Try to establish their own position within the team ❑

7. One of the key reasons for a virtual team meeting is:
   - a) To stave off the boredom which members feel when working alone ❑
   - b) To help team members avoid a feeling of dissociation from the rest of the team ❑
   - c) To ensure that the team members are actually doing some work ❑
   - d) To give them a chance to gossip ❑

8. What's the biggest danger in attending a meeting at which your expertise is sought?
   - a) That you have simply been invited to ratify a silly decision ❑
   - b) That your expertise will be ignored ❑
   - c) That you will disagree with others who share different opinions ❑
   - d) That you don't know your subject sufficiently well ❑

9. A meeting whose purpose is for a group to make a decision collaboratively is most appropriate when:
a) Individuals are scared of taking individual responsibility for a decision and so need group support ❑
b) The team members are not clever enough to make decisions on their own ❑
c) It would be commercially unwise for one person to make the decision alone ❑
d) It is important for team members to believe that the organization is democratic ❑

10. Which two ideas should you constantly review as a professional person?
a) Stewardship and legality ❑
b) Stewardship and legacy ❑
c) Stewardship and legitimacy ❑
d) Stewardship and leadership ❑

SUNDAY
MONDAY
TUESDAY
WEDNESDAY
THURSDAY
FRIDAY
SATURDAY

MONDAY

Preparing for a meeting

You may have experienced being asked to attend a meeting whose purpose is unclear and wondering why you were invited at all. The key to a successful meeting is careful planning and thoughtful preparation.

Preparation may be the responsibility of either the Chair of the meeting or a participant. Some Chairs actively prepare for meetings and some delegate the responsibilities to others. With an increasing trend in rotating the chairing of meetings, it's quite likely that you will be called upon to prepare a meeting at any stage in your career.

Today we'll look at everything you need to do to make a meeting work. Meticulous planning at this stage reaps rewards in terms of meeting success. Participants who are able to find their way easily to a venue, are made to feel welcome (or, at the least, expected) when they arrive and feel that some thought has gone into the organization of the meeting (or, at the least, do not notice any problems) tend to contribute more.

We'll call those attending a meeting 'participants' and not 'attendees', which suggests someone attended to rather than taking an active part, or 'delegates', which implies that someone has delegated their attendance. Ideally, meeting participants should attend through choice!

SUNDAY

MONDAY

TUESDAY

WEDNESDAY

THURSDAY

FRIDAY

SATURDAY

Starting with purpose

Start your preparation by determining the purpose of the meeting:

- Why and by whom is it believed to be necessary?
- What are the intended outcomes?
- Is it time critical?
- What will happen if it fails to meet its objectives?
- What might contribute to its success?

The agenda

The agenda sets out the purpose of the meeting (if the participants don't already know), the topics to be discussed, who leads on each topic and usually some logistical arrangements which may be reiterated in a separate invitation. It is worthwhile including them as an additional page in the agenda because busy people often neglect to print invitations and may miss important details such as venue and timing.

The agenda should list all participants and any special roles they will have in the meeting.

Here's a sample template for an agenda:

- Meeting subject
- Meeting objectives
- Meeting organizer (with contact details)
- Meeting recorder
- Names of invited participants
- Venue, date and time
- Pre-meeting reading
- Apologies for absence
- Action points and matters arising from last meeting
- Specific topics to be discussed, with brief detail, topic owners and allotted timings
- Details of next meeting

Let's look at each item in turn. The first items are all scene setters, designed to give background information to those attending:

- Meeting subject
  - For example: Meeting of the finance subcommittee to determine the level of funding for the new wing of Cell Block H.
- Meeting objectives
  - For example: 'We are charged with allocating funds towards completion of the new building. All budgets must be completed by 3 March and so it is vital that we reach

our final decision at this meeting to get budget approval.' This, combined with the meeting subject, is our statement of purpose.

- Meeting organizer (with contact details)
  - The name of the meeting owner. It may be the Chair, the Chair's personal assistant, one of the participants or another interested party. Include telephone and e-mail details and a title or role – something to make clear the involvement of this person to participants who may not recognize the name.
- Meeting recorder
  - The name of the person who will record the significant points arising from the meeting.
- Names of invited participants
  - Participants like to know who else will attend a meeting so they can prepare properly for it. Would you prepare more or less rigorously if you had to present an argument designed to influence your friends or your organization's Board of Directors?
- Venue, date and time
  - Where the meeting will be and when. We'll look at venue and timing in more detail shortly.
- Pre-meeting reading
  - Any essential background reading. Ensure that you send the background material when you send out the agenda.

The second set of items outline what will happen, in sequence, during the meeting:

- Apologies for absence
  - It's usual to record who has notified the Chair of their absence before the meeting. This way they can be eliminated from the list of unexplained absentees who should be contacted after the meeting to explain their absence.
- Action points and matters arising from last meeting
  - The best Chair, as we'll see on Wednesday, follows up on action points to ensure that they have been completed. In this part of the meeting, participants briefly describe how they have tackled the actions to which they agreed at the last meeting. It's also a place to raise any serious issues

which demanded thought from the participants after the
last meeting.
- Specific topics to be discussed, with brief detail, topic owners
and allotted timings
  - How many topics to include in an agenda is a matter
    of judgement. The list must be manageable within the
    allotted time. You will have to make your best guess
    at how long a topic will take based on, for example, the
    complexity and critical nature of a topic, the level of
    interest and knowledge of the participants and other local
    factors. If in doubt, reduce the number of topics on the
    agenda to be safe.
- Arrange/announce details of next meeting

Any other business?

No! Notice that the traditional item, any other business (AOB),
is not included here. Meetings must be purposeful and AOB
dilutes that purpose.

AOB has long been an excuse by the vocal minority to
hijack a meeting, using it as a platform to address their own
political agendas or introduce topics they were too lazy to
bring to the attention of the meeting organizer before the
meeting. Often the person who raises other business is the
least prepared for the meeting. In reality, many meetings
spend longer discussing other business than dealing with
scheduled topics.

The absence of AOB has several benefits:

1 The meeting remains purposeful and on topic.
2 The meeting can run to time. AOB can create long
  extensions to a meeting.
3 Everyone is open with each other about the meeting.
4 There can be no surprises. Meeting participants should have
  time to prepare for a topic before the meeting, and AOB
  prevents that preparation. The only person likely to be prepared
  to discuss the other business is the person who raises the
  topic, and there is a considerable danger of them railroading
  participants into agreement with something which they have not
  considered in sufficient detail to make an informed decision.

The only reason for other business to be discussed comes when an emergency arises between the distribution of the agenda and the meeting date. If this is the case, the person involved should raise the issue with the Chair and, if sufficient people see the urgent need to discuss it, then it can be included. Do not ever include AOB in the agenda, because participants should use it as a rare exception and not a rule.

Determining who should be invited

If you are inviting people to a regular meeting of a standing committee, then the cast list will change little between meetings. If it is a one-off meeting it becomes a little trickier. Sometimes we invite too many people for fear of causing offence if we don't invite them. If in doubt, take advice about who should be invited. Too many participants make discussions long and decision-making difficult. If you invite too few, they or others may complain that certain interests are not represented and so the meeting has no real authority to make an informed decision. Try to find people representing each key interest, argument or viewpoint for the major topics being discussed. See who has attended similar meetings in the past, ask the Chairs of other meetings for their recommendations and ask those whom you know should attend if there is anyone vital missing from the list.

The invitation to the meeting

Nowadays we tend to e-mail rather than post meeting agendas, unless there are hard copies of background reading to be included. The agenda is often an attachment to an e-mail inviting participants to attend. Your invitations should:

1 Reiterate the subject, date, time and venue of the meeting. Typically, where budget allows, you would invite participants for coffee around 30 minutes before the official start of the meeting. In most cultures, the social chat before the meeting is important.
2 Make clear what background reading participants must do before attending. Attach the reading where possible.

3 Ask participants to take note of who is expected to address which topics.

4 Mention dress code if this is important or not known/obvious to participants.

5 Provide travel and parking arrangements. Use online mapping services to embed a map, directions and details of parking and public transport links within your invitations.

6 Give contact details, including an emergency number to phone if you have difficulty getting to the meeting on the day.

7 Ask about special dietary requirements if you intend to feed the participants.

8 Ask participants who intend to use slides or other supporting materials to send them before the meeting so that they can be copied for other participants. If it's important that the other participants read them before the event, then ask that the materials be circulated a working week before the meeting.

9 Ask participants to confirm their attendance by a set date, giving your contact details for their reply. This is important, if only for catering purposes!

> There is a certain wisdom in the idea that the further someone has to travel, the earlier they will arrive and vice-versa. If half of your meeting participants have travelled some distance to a venue and the other half are local, it's likely that the locals will arrive later.
>
> I recently attended a meeting in a large government building. The participants were all from one team, based in another part of the same building. Many of the participants arrived late, explaining that they had never been in this part of the building before and couldn't find their way around. I had travelled more than 250 km to attend the meeting and arrived half an hour before the first in-house participant.

Choosing a venue

In practice, you will select a venue before completing the agenda and sending out the invitations. Here are some things you may want to consider in choosing a venue:

1 familiarity
   - Have you/the participants used the venue before?
2 location

   - Is the location onsite or offsite? Onsite is familiar and easy. Everyone knows where everything is and you have access to telephones, copiers and in-house expertise. It's also easier to gain access to the in-house computer network. However, participants may find the proximity of colleagues distracting and, if the meeting is on the participants' own office premises, you'll find that getting them back to the meeting after breaks is difficult because 'I'll just go and check my e-mails' leads to people disappearing from the meeting ('to sort out an urgent issue') and either not returning or missing important parts of the meeting. Meeting offsite may give participants a greater sense of the importance or seriousness of a meeting because they can see the investment in it. External catering may offer a refreshing change. Because it's more difficult for participants to check e-mails and disappear to their desks, you may find they get more involved. However, it will inevitably be more expensive than running a meeting in-house. Most organizations don't pay their employees' travel costs from home to work but do pay for travel to external venues. Check that you have sufficient budget to cover all the costs of an outside venue.

- How close is it to the base locations of the invited participants? Are you asking participants to travel further to the venue than they would to work? Early starts and bad traffic or unpleasant public transport breed tiredness and bad feeling, and ideally you want to start any meeting with participants who are wide awake and in good spirits
- How easy is it to find?
- Is it close to public transport links?

3 space required
- How many people need to be accommodated? Is the room sufficiently large? Is there space between and behind the chairs? If the meeting is likely to be long, are the chairs (too) comfortable?

4 equipment
- If projectors and/or sound equipment are required, can the venue provide them or should you bring your own? Can they supply four-block power supplies so that you can plug in equipment? Can they supply rubber masking or duct tape to ensure that you have no trailing wires? Can they provide flipcharts and pens? Insist on dark-coloured flipchart markers – whiteboard markers are useless on paper and red and green ink is difficult to read at any distance from the flipchart.

5 catering arrangements
- Do not over-cater. People work better hungry than full!
- Ensure that the caterers are able to meet any special dietary requirements.

6 seating arrangements
- Can you arrange the seating so that the appropriate people sit together/apart according to office politics, relationships and other sensitivities?

7 ease of access based on participants' base locations
8 ease and cost of parking
   - Check your budgets. Many city-based car parks charge
     punitive amounts for a few hours' parking.

Tell the venue administrators the name of your meeting and
organization, who is attending and the room number. Ask
them to put up signage showing your participants how to get
to the room.

Check on the security arrangements. Do participants need
passes to move between sections of the building? There is little
more aggravating (and, for some, embarrassing) than having
to ask someone resident in a building to accompany them to
the toilet because the toilet area is behind a door requiring
an electronic security pass. Plead the case for temporary
security passes for your participants and they will have a more
comfortable day.

Timing and sequencing of a meeting

If you plan to start the meeting late in the morning, consider
whether or not you will need to arrange a working lunch in the
middle or whether it is appropriate to break off for lunch.

If you plan an afternoon meeting, will you provide lunch
first? Will the meeting finish in time to allow those travelling
some distance to get home at a reasonable hour?

People tend to work better before a meal than after. Thus,
you may want to sequence the agenda topics so that the more
difficult discussions take place before lunch.

Accommodation

If people have to stay overnight before or after a meeting,
ensure that you/they have the budget to do so. It is courteous if
you are the owner or organizer of a meeting to book overnight
accommodation on behalf of your participants. If you do so,
make sure that they are aware of the payment arrangements –
have you paid in advance, or guaranteed the room for them
to settle the bill on arrival or departure? Your organization

may have an agreed lower rate in certain hotels and an upper spending limit for accommodation and meals.
Check:

- the proximity of the accommodation to the venue
- the cost of the room
- which meals, if any, are included in the room rate
- whether WiFi is available (and, more importantly, whether it is free). Increasingly people want to work in hotels and easy and free access to WiFi within their bedrooms rather than in public areas makes their stay more comfortable (and productive).

Send participants a map showing both the meeting venue and the overnight accommodation, indicating the distance between the two and how to get from one to the other.

Preparing participants for the meeting

It may be useful to talk to participants who are expected to present at the meeting to ensure that they understand the purpose of the meeting and the reason why they should present. Reiterate the timing of their topic – both the start time and the duration – and check that they are comfortable about what they have been asked to do.

Summary

Every meeting should have a clear purpose which is known and understood by the participants. The agenda should combine scene-setting information and a running order and should exclude 'Any other business'. Send invitations only to those who can make a valid contribution to the meeting's purpose, and, in writing the invitation, consider the question 'What would I want to know if I were being invited to this meeting?' Use the checklist in this chapter to ensure that the venue is fit for purpose and think carefully about the timing and sequencing of the meeting. Remember that some participants may need overnight accommodation before or after the meeting, and remember to brief anyone who is expected to present at the meeting.

SUNDAY

MONDAY

TUESDAY

WEDNESDAY

THURSDAY

FRIDAY

SATURDAY

Fact-check (answers at the back)

1. The starting point in preparing for a meeting is:
   a) Determining the purpose of the meeting ❑
   b) Sending out invitations ❑
   c) Deciding who should come ❑
   d) Writing the agenda ❑

2. Any other business (AOB):
   a) Should usually be included in an agenda ❑
   b) Should always be included in an agenda ❑
   c) Should be an optional extra in an agenda ❑
   d) Should generally be excluded from an agenda ❑

3. People tend to work better:
   a) Before lunch ❑
   b) After lunch ❑
   c) Over a working lunch ❑
   d) Without lunch ❑

4. The role of the meeting recorder is:
   a) To record the meeting so those not attending can hear what happened ❑
   b) To make notes of significant points arising from the meeting ❑
   c) To write down everything that is said, verbatim ❑
   d) To collect evidence which may be used against meeting participants ❑

5. It can be useful to hold meetings away from the workplace because:
   a) It reduces distractions, like e-mail and interruptions from colleagues ❑
   b) It is cheaper ❑
   c) It's nice to get away for the day ❑
   d) Hotels and conference centres have better meeting rooms ❑

6. It is useful to brief participants who are going to address a topic at the meeting because:
   a) They need to know that you will be on their side in the meeting ❑
   b) They need to know the politics surrounding the issue ❑
   c) It gives them the option to decline the invitation to the meeting ❑
   d) They need to understand the purpose and timing ❑

7. You should inform the administrators at an external venue of the name of your meeting, your organization and your participants so that:
   a) They can meet, greet and guide people to the meeting room ❑
   b) They can boast in their marketing literature that your organization is their client ❑
   c) They can have coffee and croissants ready for your arrival ❑
   d) They can prepare name badges in advance of the meeting ❑

8. Check on the corporate spending limits for meals and accommodation so that:
a) Participants can make sure they spend up to the limit ☐
b) Participants can make sure that they don't overspend ☐
c) Participants feel guilty that you are spending money on them ☐
d) You can catch participants out if their expense claims are too high ☐

9. When you send an invitation to a meeting:
a) Simply include an address – people should be able to find their own way to the venue ☐
b) Tell people to ask directions when they get close to the venue, because it may be tricky to find ☐
c) Just give them a postcode so they can use satellite navigation to find the venue ☐
d) Include a map and directions to help people to find the venue ☐

10. When determining who should be invited to a meeting:
a) Err on the side of inviting too many, because that way you won't offend anyone by missing them off the list ☐
b) Err on the side of 'less is more' and invite the smallest number possible to keep the meeting short ☐
c) Take advice if you are unsure about who can best contribute ☐
d) Invite the people who can tell a good story and will entertain the others ☐

SUNDAY

MONDAY

TUESDAY

WEDNESDAY

THURSDAY

FRIDAY

SATURDAY

TUESDAY

Participating in a meeting

As a participant in a meeting you have rather more to do than simply turn up!

If you attend a meeting and say nothing, then you have contributed nothing to the meeting's success.

If you dominate the meeting, whether or not you have more of use to offer than some of the other participants, then the meeting served little point other than as a platform for you to air your views, and others will question their own attendance and may resent you.

You may be nervous about contributing, feeling that others have more experience, more seniority or more useful things to offer than you.

You may be bored by the meeting and subconsciously display signs of your boredom to others.

Today we'll look at the skills you need to get the best out of a meeting and to contribute most effectively to its success. We'll start with a self-assessment and use it as the basis for much of what follows. Answer each question honestly – answering quickly will yield a more truthful view than answering slowly. When you have completed the assessment, read the analysis below to see what your score signifies.

While the assessment carries no scientific rigour, it will indicate the areas in which some development would yield rewards for you.

Your participant skills	1 Never	2 Occasionally	3 Frequently	4 Always
I am comfortable in meetings, greetings and social talk before a meeting begins				
I am a good listener and genuinely interested in the answers others give to my questions				
I allow others to finish making their point before I speak				
I am confident when making a point or stating my views				
I am concise and articulate in stating my case in a meeting				
I'm good at reading and understanding others' body language				
I'm aware of my own body language and how others may interpret it				
My body language suggests engagement and self-confidence				
I am able to assert myself when I have something useful to say				
I am able to concede when I am wrong				
I can control the tone of my voice when I feel nervous or anxious				
I dress appropriately for each meeting I attend				
I listen carefully to what other people are saying in a meeting				
I am thoroughly prepared for every meeting I attend				
I know what my objectives are before I attend a meeting				
I always do the background reading required of me before a meeting				
I carefully review the notes of the previous meeting				
I research in advance the views of the other participants at a meeting				
I share a common purpose with the other participants at a meeting				
If a meeting is not relevant to me, I will not attend				
Totals				

Analysis	
20–39	You have a lot of work to do to develop your participant skills. Make sure that you understand what is expected of you when you accept an invitation to a meeting, do the background preparation and make sure that you contribute actively and appropriately
40–59	You have the basic participant skills and now it's time to hone them so that you can contribute even more effectively
60–80	Your meeting skills are good. Now it's time to turn them from good to excellent

Before the meeting

Do your homework:

1 Discover why the meeting is taking place – what is its purpose?
2 Find out who owns it.
3 Do the background reading.
4 Pick up on topics which are of particular interest or relevance to you and decide whether there are particular contributions you want to make to them.
5 Check how to get to the venue and how long it will take you.
6 Double-check the timing.
7 Check the dress code.

The social aspect of a meeting

Meetings, greetings and business cards

You arrive 20 minutes before the start of a meeting. Other participants are starting to congregate. Some are familiar and some are new to you. It's time to introduce yourself.

Do not underestimate meetings and greetings. We form impressions of others within 5–7 seconds of meeting them and, whether or not they are accurate, others will treat us as though their impression of us is true. Did you ever meet someone whom you disliked at first and then grew to like? Or perhaps you liked someone at first and then grew to dislike them? Either way, your first impressions were wrong. Unfortunately, most of us will act as though they are right, rather than suspending our judgement until we get to know someone a little better. The way in which you meet and greet someone counts enormously towards their perception of your credibility. If they like you on first meeting they are more likely to be sympathetic towards the views you express. If they dislike you, they are more likely to attack your views or, at best, not take you very seriously.

Let's start with handshakes. When you shake someone's hand, grasp their hand in yours with a flat palm and a firm grip, and shake their hand up and down two or three times. Do not offer your hand to be shaken – a handshake is an active greeting, not a passive display of submission. Equally, do not offer your fingers – there is little more unpleasant to someone with a good, firm handshake than to be offered a set of fingers to waggle.

A weak handshake sends out the wrong signals. It puts you on the back foot with a domineering or aggressive person, who, whether consciously or subconsciously, will see you as a person they can dominate or bully.

As you shake hands, smile at the other person, look them in the eyes and make sure that your eyebrows are momentarily raised and lowered. Socially functional people (and chimpanzees) flash their eyebrows in a fraction of a second on greeting others. Socially dysfunctional people (and chimps) keep their eyebrows still.

As you smile and flash your eyebrows, give your name – twice! For example, I would say 'Hello, I'm David – David Cotton'. When people meet for the first time, they are often focused inwards, worrying about how they appear to others. For this reason, they tend not to hear others' names properly on introduction. If you say your first name, then your entire name, it will sound entirely natural and double the chances that they will remember who you are. It's then easier, and less embarrassing, for them when they come to introduce you to others, to remember your name and introduce you without having to say 'I'm sorry, I didn't catch your name'.

Listen to other people's names and repeat a name as you hear it, to help you to remember it. For example, if someone says 'Hi, I'm Pat', say 'Hello, Pat, it's nice to meet you'.

Many people claim to be poor at remembering others' names on first meeting. In reality, many of us are so focused on ourselves and the impression that we are creating that we don't listen well when others tell us their names.

Try this. When someone introduces themselves, tell them it's nice to meet them and use their name – 'It's very nice to meet you, Ahmed'. Then mentally repeat their name to yourself several times as you look at them and listen to them talking. As you meet the next person, do the same again, then glance back at the first person and ensure that you still remember their name. This simple repetition of the name, once out loud and several times silently, with a few checks back to each person you have met, will help you remember many names.

When the meeting starts, if you are able to address people by name, your credibility will rise. Remembering someone's name first time sends a message that they were important enough to you to merit you remembering them, which is very flattering to them.

Here's an interesting quirk for you. When two men meet socially or in a business setting, they should always stand slightly angled to each other. If a man greets another face on, it feels as though they are 'squaring up' to each other and gives the impression of being confrontational. When a man and a woman meet, they should stand facing each other. If a man angles himself towards a woman it will feel as though he is 'sidling up' and has another agenda. Two woman are generally comfortable either angled or face to face and will often stand closer to each other, even on first greeting, than two men or a man and woman. These little things make a big difference to others' level of comfort with you. And from that comfort comes credibility.

If you exchange business cards after the initial greetings, make sure you know something of the culture of the people you are meeting. In Japan, for example, business cards are generally offered and received with two hands, studied and then left on the table in front of the recipient during a meeting. In Western society, cards tend to be offered and received one-handed, briefly studied and then pocketed.

Seating

Ask the Chair if there is a seating plan. If there is none, sit where you can catch the eye of the Chair easily, so you can indicate clearly when you want to speak. Be tidy, putting your briefcase or computer bag out of the way and ensuring that you have all the paperwork, pens and other equipment you need in front of you when the meeting starts.

Presence

Switch off all your toys – mobile phones, BlackBerrys, computers, iPods, iPads and anything else which has an off switch – and put them out of sight. If you are serious about attending this meeting, then you should demonstrate that you are present. A communications device on the table in front of you will simply distract you, which is discourteous to other participants, suggesting that your work is more important than the meeting in hand.

Knowing who's who

If there are several people around the table who are unfamiliar to you, it's worth sketching a table plan and noting their names. Knowing others' names will give you more confidence to address them.

Listening

Now the meeting has started, it's time to listen. Are you a good listener? Are you hearing what is actually being said or what you expect someone to say?

Scribble some brief notes as you listen to others speaking, so you can address directly what they said rather than something half-remembered or misattributed.

Reading people

William Glasser,[5] an eminent psychiatrist, says that from around puberty until death we will have, hard-wired into our brains, certain drivers of behaviour and we will seek out those things which meet the needs of our drivers. If we find them, we will tend to be happy and contented. If we do not, we will tend towards unhappiness and discontent.

There are five drivers:

- love and belonging
- power and status
- freedom
- fun
- survival.

Most of us will have one as a primary driver of our behaviour and another as a secondary driver. The other drivers will be less important to us. While we may have a temporary shift to a different driver according to situation, most of us will seek to fulfil our primary and secondary drivers throughout our lives.

The five drivers are relatively easy to spot in others and, once we know them, we can treat them like 'hot buttons' to press in order to get the best out of them and out of our relationships with them.

Let's look at the characteristics of these drivers:

1 *Love and belonging.* People with this driver tend to be drawn towards teamwork, seeking out the camaraderie of others and feeling uncomfortable and isolated if they cannot work in a team. In meetings, you will see them seeking consensus and wanting to be sure that others agree and approve of any ideas that they put forward.

2 *Power and status.* People with this driver want recognition. They want to stand out from the crowd. In meetings you'll see them airing views contrary to those expressed by others because immediate agreement may suggest that they don't know their own mind and would bring them down to the same level as the other participants. Don't be subservient to them, but openly acknowledge their ideas. If you have a good idea, even if you are certain that it is right, suggest that this is something you wanted to bounce off the others and then look at the person driven by power and status and ask them directly '[Name], what do you think?' They will find something to change, but are more likely to accept your idea because you flattered them by asking them first.

3 *Freedom.* People driven by freedom want autonomy. They feel constrained by rules and are uncomfortable with processes.

Give them the space to create ideas and be careful in the language you use to address them, avoiding statements like 'you must' and 'the rules state...'. Do not expect them to be 'teamy', but tap into their potential for great creativity. If you can engage them and get them on your side, they can provide a wealth of new ideas unconstrained by 'the way we do things around here'.

4 *Fun.* People driven by fun may seem the most difficult to work with because their primary driving force is enjoyment and others may take a meeting extremely seriously. Fun people will make jokes, appear to deviate from the subject under discussion and give the impression of not taking anything seriously. In reality, they are listening very closely to what others say – they have to in order to find the fun in it. Like the traditional Shakespearean 'fool', they are able to see through pomposity and starchiness and get to the nub of an issue very quickly. Fun and humour are creative and, if you channel their creativity, you'll see that they have a lot to contribute to a meeting.

5 *Survival.* At its basic level, you are unlikely to meet people at work with survival as their primary driver, because it's about not knowing where your next meal will come from or whether you will have a roof over your head tonight. However, each of us can switch to another driver temporarily as our life circumstances change, and you may well meet people who feel concerned for their livelihood, threatened in their jobs or generally uncomfortable with their current position who will display the behaviours of someone driven by survival. Treat them kindly, but not patronisingly. Be factual without being harsh.

Knowing when to speak and asserting yourself

When you first join a committee or working group, or find yourself in a corporate meeting, it's easy to think that everyone else knows more than you, has more experience and therefore has more valid contributions to make. Step back from this for a moment: you were invited to the meeting, and so you have a right to be there. If you sit in silence you may learn a great deal but you will have contributed nothing and may not get a repeat invitation. Most people around the meeting table are happy to accept you as a valid member of the group with something to say. You have a right to speak and a right to be heard.

One of the best ways of speaking at a meeting if you are a little nervous is to ask a question. Don't worry about sounding silly or naive. When someone else speaks, say, for example, 'Tell me a little more about that' or 'I'm not familiar with that – would you mind expanding on it?'. Generally the person you address will be pleased to say more, and you will have made your first contribution.

Knowing when to speak can be difficult. In formal meetings, contributions are made through the Chair and people motion to the Chair that they wish to speak. An astute Chair should be looking for non-verbal signs that people want to contribute and invite comments if they know that you have expertise in a particular area. In less formal meetings, it's usually a free for all in which you get to speak by jumping in at an opportune moment. In the early stages, notice how other people successfully indicate that they want to speak and then follow their lead.

Be bold when you speak. Avoid apologies and do not play the 'I'm the new kid on the block' game for too long because this will annoy seasoned meeting-goers. Clearly and audibly say what you have to say. Stick to the point. If you want to make a bold assertion, it can be useful to start it with 'In my own experience...'. Your own experience is incontrovertible – whether or not others agree with your point, they cannot argue with your experience!

Presenting within a meeting

Sometimes you will be asked to make a short presentation within a meeting. Be concise and argue your case or make your key points very clearly. If you have the chance to prepare beforehand, it's useful to have a structure for your presentation.

Presentations have a beginning ('Tell them what you're going to tell them'), a middle ('Tell them') and an end ('Tell them what you told them'. Do not introduce more than two or three key themes and do not overrun. Nobody will mind if your presentation is shorter than the allocated time.

There's a useful mnemonic to help you structure the introduction to a presentation. Although designed for longer presentations, it can be adapted for a shorter presentation. Remember 'INTRO':

Interest/impact
Needs
Timing
Range
Objectives

Interest/impact: grab people's attention right at the beginning with an interesting statement or, better still, a question that makes them sit up and listen. Avoid telling them your name and saying 'I'm here to talk about xyz' – be interesting!

Needs: a simple statement which indicates why they should need to listen to you.

Timing: how long you plan to speak.

Range: the themes you will cover.

Objectives: what the participants will take away with them at the end.

Here's an example. Imagine you lead a team that sells widgets and are addressing the sales team at their regular meeting:

(Interest/impact) 'Welcome! Last week we bid for one of the biggest contracts in our history. It would have netted us 15 million euros. Our sales manager, George Brown – alas no longer with us as of Friday – led the bid. (Need) Had George understood that the tendering company wanted both widgets and wodgets, he might have been here today to share his success. Unfortunately, George had immersed himself in the wonderful world of widgets and knew little about our company's other

> offerings, and so was unable to cross-sell them. (Timing)
> Over the next 20 minutes, (Range) I'm going to introduce
> you to the humble wodget, how it's made, what it looks like
> and our pricing structure so that (Objective) you will feel
> rather more comfortable than our friend George in cross-
> selling our products and be able to come back and share
> your triumphs with us.'

Many of us will feel reasonably confident sitting down but less
so standing up. Our brain sends out a rush of adrenaline as a
protective mechanism, and this adrenaline allows us to fight
or run away from the thing which frightens us (the 'fight or
flight' syndrome). Because we can neither beat up the other
meeting participants nor run away from them, we are left with
the side-effects of undissipated adrenaline, which may include
a dry mouth, butterflies in the stomach and shaky hands and
legs. You can reduce your nerves through good preparation,
rehearsal, a little deep breathing, making notes of keywords
and breathing deeply before you start. Do not have a cold drink
because it tends to tighten your vocal cords and your voice will
sound strained. A warm drink is better. The more practice you
have, the easier it becomes.

Summary

You have a right to attend a meeting and you are expected to contribute. If you know the purpose of a meeting, you can make a reasonable guess about why your experience is relevant and therefore what is expected of you at the meeting.

Do all the background reading and ensure that you have taken all the actions assigned to you at an earlier meeting.

Rather than go along with prepared speeches, think about the points you would like to make and, when the chance comes, indicate that you want to talk and make your points. There is nothing worse than thinking after a meeting 'I wish I had said something at that point'.

SUNDAY
MONDAY
TUESDAY
WEDNESDAY
THURSDAY
FRIDAY
SATURDAY

Meet and greet with confidence, listening to and repeating others' names and giving your own clearly, twice.

When the meeting starts, listen and observe. Notice the level of formality or informality and act at that level. See what drives others' behaviour and use that in responding to them so that they can see that you understand them, even if you don't agree with them. Be free from distractions.

Above all, remember that you have a right to contribute and your contributions are as valid and valuable as anyone else's.

Fact-check (answers at the back)

1. When meeting and greeting:
   a) We form impressions of others in around a minute ☐
   b) We form impressions of others in around 30 seconds ☐
   c) We form impressions of others in 5–7 seconds ☐
   d) We form impressions in around 2 seconds ☐

2. Our first impressions:
   a) May be wrong ☐
   b) Are invariably right ☐
   c) Are always wrong ☐
   d) Don't matter ☐

3. Having your phone on during a meeting:
   a) Is perfectly acceptable. As a professional, you are expected to multitask ☐
   b) Sends out a signal that you have more important business to attend to than the meeting ☐
   c) Sends out a signal that you are important and boosts your credibility among the meeting participants ☐
   d) Relieves the tedium of the meeting ☐

4. Sketching a table plan:
   a) Will help you to remember where you were sitting when you return from a break ☐
   b) Is a useful distraction during a boring meeting ☐
   c) Is generally a waste of time ☐
   d) Helps you to know who's who so you can address them with more confidence ☐

5. Glasser's five behavioural drivers are:
   a) Love and belonging, power and status, freedom, fun and survival ☐
   b) Love and belonging, money, freedom, fun and survival ☐
   c) Love and belonging, power and status, recognition, fun and survival ☐
   d) Love and belonging, power and achievement, reward, fun and survival ☐

6. One of the best ways to talk for the first time in a meeting is:
   a) To make a bold assertion ☐
   b) To ask a question ☐
   c) To interrupt the most vocal participant ☐
   d) To ask the other participants if they would mind you speaking ☐

7. When you speak for the first time at a meeting:
   a) Apologize ☐
   b) Start by saying that you really don't know much about the topic ☐
   c) Be relatively aggressive to establish your right to speak ☐
   d) Do not apologize ☐

8. In the INTRO mnemonic, which helps you to introduce a presentation, 'I' stands for:
   a) Instruction/information ☐
   b) Information/interest ☐
   c) Interest/impact ☐
   d) Instruction/impact ☐

9. If you are nervous about speaking:
a) Have a drink of cold water ❏
b) Have a warm drink ❏
c) Do not drink anything ❏
d) Drink a small amount of alcohol before the meeting ❏

10. When you go into the meeting room:
a) Check whether there is a seating plan ❏
b) Sit wherever you are most comfortable ❏
c) As a courtesy, let everyone else sit down first and take the remaining seat ❏
d) Sit nearest to the door so that you can leave early if the meeting is boring ❏

WEDNESDAY

Chairing a meeting

Without a Chair to maintain some level of control, many meetings would descend into disorder. The Chair plays a crucial role in ensuring that a meeting meets its objectives. The role brings with it a certain degree of power and good deal of responsibility.

Many organizations rotate the chairing of a regular meeting, and so, even if you are relatively junior within an organization, you may be expected to chair a meeting. This chapter sets out the skills, tools and techniques which are needed for effective chairing. Let's start with the Chair's Charter – a checklist of the things which a good Chair will do, and which will set a benchmark for you as you develop your chairing experience.

We worked with a board of directors who were obsessive mobile phone users. We ran a three-day event for them and confiscated their phones, giving them to a temporary secretary who was hired to take their calls and pass on messages during breaks, when they were allowed to use their phones again.

On day one, the directors were nervous and twitchy, missing their fix.

On day two they were visibly calmer.

By day three they said that they felt like a burden had been lifted from them, and they were experiencing a new-found sense of freedom.

We heard afterwards that it became common practice in their own organization to ban phones from meeting rooms.

The Chair's Charter

- I demonstrate the behaviours that I expect from participants
- I check before the meeting that everyone has been notified of it
- I do all the appropriate background reading before a meeting
- I schedule regular meetings of the same group one year ahead
- I compile the agenda, either alone or with someone else who will be attending the meeting
- I allocate time slots to agenda items based on how critical they are, how divisive I believe the discussion will be and how many items we must cover during the meeting
- I check the action points from the last agenda and note which ones I need to deal with under 'action points from last agenda'
- I am not tolerant of failure to complete the actions agreed at the last meeting – I expect that those who agree to actions will take those actions
- I check that the air temperature in the meeting room is comfortable and that there is reasonable ventilation
- I do not sacrifice humour for the sake of seriousness, but I do expect us to work through the agenda

- I sit in a position where as many participants as possible can see me
- I start meetings absolutely on time
- I set out the purpose of the meeting at the outset and check that everyone understands it
- I check the base level of understanding of a topic before we discuss it in detail
- I do not deviate (nor allow deviation) from the meeting agenda
- I am impartial in all matters discussed in the meeting
- I listen to what is said and ask clarifying questions to ensure that everyone understands the points being expressed
- I allow everyone to be heard, whether or not I agree with their viewpoint
- I use other facilitative techniques to stimulate discussion
- I do not allow anyone to dominate the meeting, regardless of their seniority or perceived importance
- I do not allow subgroup conversations during the meeting
- I ask all participants to switch off telephones, BlackBerrys, computers and other equipment before the meeting starts
- If someone chooses to use a telephone or BlackBerry during the meeting, I stop the meeting and ask them to switch it off
- I handle disruptions calmly and patiently and will not let them spoil the meeting
- I summarize what has been said and check that I have done so fairly
- I observe participants closely and use their body language as a gauge of the pace and atmosphere of a meeting
- I ensure that agreements and action points are recorded
- I encourage quiet participants if I believe that they can make a useful contribution
- I check that everyone knows the actions they must take following the meeting
- I finish every meeting exactly on time – I have a reputation for working to time

It's a long list and some of the elements require considerable skill and diplomacy.

Let's look at some of these in more detail:

Demonstrating what I expect from others

The Chair's role is a leadership role and, in any leadership position, what you do and say gives permission for everyone else to do and say the same things. You must be a role model for good conduct at all stages before, during and after the meeting.

Checking action points from the last meeting

One of the early agenda items is 'actions from the last meeting'. If people do not undertake the agreed actions, then there was no point to the meeting. Meetings are undertaken to produce results of some kind, and you should politely indicate that you are not tolerant of failure to take those actions. Even less forgivable is a failure to notify you or others before the meeting of the reasons why you have not undertaken those actions.

Starting on time

A meeting is said to be 'quorate' when an agreed minimum number of people have arrived at the allotted start time and 'inquorate' when they have not. If you are chairing a fairly regular meeting, find out what number makes the meeting quorate and, if you have the required minimum at the start time, then begin.

You have no obligation to help late arrivals catch up. As a role model you should demonstrate and encourage punctuality.

Purpose and understanding

At the start of the meeting, welcome everyone and state the reason for the meeting. At the start of each new agenda topic, check that everyone understands the topic, its importance and the background to it. Very often a small number of people will debate something hotly and, when the Chair asks for other contributions, someone will shyly admit that they did not really understand what was being discussed.

Make sure that you have done all the necessary background reading before the meeting. Put someone on the spot, asking them for their comments on a background paper. This will demonstrate what you expect of others when you chair the meeting. If they are embarrassed because they have not done the background reading, that's their problem!

Keeping on track

It's easy to get side-tracked in a meeting. A chance remark can lead everyone away from the topic and the meeting loses its way. One of your jobs as Chair is to bring everything back on track. Do it gently (at least at first), suggesting 'We seem to have drifted away from the topic in hand', and use it as an opportunity to summarize the discussions up to that point. Then invite someone to continue.

Ensure, too, that you stick to the agenda throughout.

Impartiality

You must remain impartial during a meeting even if everything inside you is screaming out that the opinions you are hearing are wrong. If you show bias towards a particular side in an argument then it will seriously damage your credibility.

Allow everyone an equal opportunity to speak even if you disagree fundamentally with their viewpoint.

Facilitation skills

If a meeting is designed to create new ideas, then it's useful to have some facilitation skills to draw on rather than addressing every agenda item by discussion and debate only.

> A colleague and I once facilitated a meeting of directors and senior managers in a major organization to determine their ten-year IT strategy. We told them that a ten-year IT strategy was not feasible, but they insisted that they had sufficient knowledge and background to achieve it.
>
> We were instructed to facilitate only and to offer no other contributions.
>
> During the meeting, the participants determined that their organizations would not introduce the internet nor embrace e-mail because each was a passing fad and would go away. True to our word we ventured no opinions. The Chair's job can sometimes be frustrating!

In traditional brainstorming, the facilitator describes the issue and the participants call out ideas for a given time period to resolve it. Each is recorded and when time is up the items are discussed and their merits are debated. This method is somewhat flawed. We solve problems best by stepping back, putting them on the backburner and engaging in other things. During this time, our subconscious continues to work on them. The answers tend to come to us when we are thinking of something unrelated to the problem in hand. Traditional brainstorming does not allow our subconscious to get to work. Brain-friendly brainstorming resolves this problem:

- Brainstorm for two minutes.
- Stop for two minutes and discuss something unrelated to the issue.
- Brainstorm for another two minutes.

You'll notice that we generate ideas for a very short time. The break in the middle allows our subconscious to continue to work on the issue, and we tend to generate more creative ideas after the break than before it.

Now we have a long list of ideas and need to debate each one to see whether it is worthwhile. Not only is this time-consuming, but people tend to be proprietorial about their own ideas, defending them even when others can see they have little merit. To quickly sift the worthwhile ideas, use 'PMI' (plus, minus, interesting). 'Plus' items are worth further consideration; 'minus' ideas are not worth further discussion; 'interesting' ideas may be useful at another time but are not strictly relevant to the current issue.

Call out each idea in turn from the list that the group has generated. Ask for a show of hands for each one. How many think that the idea is a 'plus'/a 'minus'/an 'interesting' idea. Go with the majority and mark the ideas in green for plus, red for minus and a neutral colour like black or blue for interesting. In just minutes you have created a list of ideas which are worthy of further discussion without having to control more senior or vocal people who will make more noise in support of their own ideas. In this version, democracy rules!

Force-field analyses

If you are planning a project or a change, then the force-field analysis is useful in helping you to see what may help the project/change to succeed and what may hinder it. It's a structured form of brainstorming.

Write a brief description of the central issue down the centre of a flipchart sheet, and head two columns either side as 'Helpers' and 'Blockers'. Ask participants to call out or write directly on the sheet everything they think will help the project/change to succeed and everything they believe may hinder it. Ask them to assign scores to each idea on a scale of 1–10 according to its importance. Alternatively, ask them whether each idea is a big, medium or small issue and draw arrows whose length corresponds to their rating (long, medium and small). You might like to use green for helpers and red for blockers for greater visual impact. The idea is to use this as the basis for discussion of the major stumbling blocks which need to be reduced or removed and the helpers which you may be able to capitalize on to remove some of the blockers. It's a simple and useful visual tool for sparking discussion.

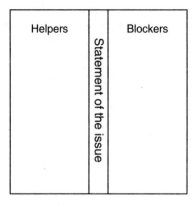

Helpers	Statement of the issue	Blockers

Difficult people and situations

The meeting hog is an attention-seeker who addresses every topic and replies to every question. Hogs stop others from having their say, and when they do say something worthwhile, it's often taken less seriously because it's seen as part of their general chatter. Because hogs want attention, one way to deal with them is to *give* them attention. When Fred is about to speak for the fifth time, say 'Come on everyone, don't make Fred do all the work!' Fred will be delighted because you have given him the attention he craves, suggesting that he is the hardest worker there. He is the only one in the room who does not realize that he has just been told to be quiet. If subtle tactics don't work, tell the hog either openly in front of the whole meeting or quietly in a break that, while you appreciate his or her level of contribution, it's really important that others have an equal say and ask him or her politely to give others a chance.

Inevitably you will encounter conflict in meetings. Two people who disagree publicly often become more heated than they would privately because they do not want to lose face.

Conflict tends to come from three main sources – professional disagreement, power struggles and personality issues. If you already have a reputation for running tightly controlled

meetings, there is a reduced chance that the conflict will become serious. If you do not, then it's time to toughen up, insisting that:

● people speak only after raising a hand
● only one person may speak at once
● everyone will be given an opportunity to contribute.

Depersonalize the conflict: if one participant says something derogatory about another, instruct them that personal comments are not appropriate. Get people to focus on 'what' they have a problem with and not 'who'.

Ask objective questions of those in conflict. Ask them what solution would make something acceptable to them.

If it's appropriate and you have the authority (and courage), it is worth talking individually to the warring factions after the meeting to get to the bottom of their issues and try to prevent a repeat of the conflict.

Summarizing

Every so often, pause the discussion and summarize. Summarizing:

● shows participants what they have achieved
● creates a natural break which may lead people to feel that the discussion has run its course
● helps participants to take stock of all the views they have heard and so make more reasoned judgements or counter-arguments.

To summarize well you have to listen well, sometimes asking clarifying questions to check your own understanding and to help others who may be reluctant to admit a lack of understanding. Make brief notes of key points rather than writing verbatim what people have said so that you can spend more time observing the group.

Observing body language

A major myth about body language is that single gestures have universal meaning. For example, many books will tell you that someone sitting with arms folded and legs crossed is feeling defensive and shutting others out. This may be true. Equally, they may be cold, or perhaps they always sit like that! What is true is that we are generally consistent in our personal use of body language, just are we are consistent in accent, dialect and word choice in our spoken language, but we will still sound different from everyone else.

Body language can tell you a lot about how people are feeling, but it's best to observe *changes* rather than continued *similarities* in body language. If someone is happy, cheerful and contributing well, with arms folded and legs crossed, then you can reasonably assume that this is just a comfortable way for them to sit. If they suddenly change their posture for reasons other than physical comfort, then you can guess that their emotional or psychological state just changed, and it's these changes that you should begin to notice. If you meet the same people regularly, pay careful attention to the words they use, their voice tone and their body language and start to notice how each aligns with the others as their moods change.

In a meeting, observe these same signs and you'll start to notice when someone wants to speak, dislikes what they are hearing, dislikes another person, or agrees or disagrees with someone else. Use these subtle clues to bring different people into the discussion at the most appropriate time, gently silence the person who is aggravating others and offer a chance to speak to someone who is reluctant to assert themselves.

Recording the meeting

One of your jobs as Chair is to ensure that significant outcomes are recorded. Ask someone before the meeting to act as recorder and tell them what you would like them to note.

Traditionally, 'minutes', a blow-by-blow record of proceedings, were taken, and in some government circles and organizations where an audit trail or public record is needed, this is still commonplace. For the most part, people find minutes boring and simply skim through them, looking for their own name or agreed actions.

In most organizations, only action points are recorded. Action points are the specific actions which people are to take as a result of the meeting and should exclude opinions, interpretations (unless agreed by all) and anything judgemental.

The recorder should note:

1 the agreed action
2 who has agreed to take the action
3 when they have agreed to do (or at least begin) it
4 anyone else whose involvement is needed to make the action possible.

At the end of the meeting, the Chair should ask the recorder to read back the actions and check that they are a fair summary of what has been agreed.

Ensure that action points are distributed within four days of the meeting.

Drawing out quiet participants

If you sense that someone has something useful to say but is reluctant to speak, make a point of smiling and nodding in their direction as someone else is talking, both to show that you are aware of them and to hint that you are about to invite them to speak. Say, for example, 'Linda – I think you have something to add here...?' Always thank new members of a group or reluctant speakers for their contributions to let them know that what they have said is fine and to encourage them to contribute more.

Closing a meeting

At the end of a meeting, you may choose to ask people to evaluate the meeting (more of this on Friday). Ask the recorder to read back the agreed actions and amend them if necessary. Agree the date of the next meeting if appropriate. Thank people for attending and contributing and tell them you look forward to seeing them again.

Summary

The Chair has a vital role in making meetings work. As Chair, you are owner, organizer, facilitator, mediator and the only impartial person at the meeting. You set the tone for the meeting and dictate and demonstrate the commitment and professionalism you expect from others. If you play your role well, people will feel that their presence and contributions are valued and the meeting will be a motivating experience.

From the outset, imagine that you have just been invited to a meeting. What would make it work for you? Think through the participants' experience right from the start – from receiving an invitation, through the meeting itself to follow-up after the meeting. What are the big things that must be right? What are the little niceties that could make it a more pleasant experience? What can you do which, if you get it right, people may not even notice but if you get it wrong they will? What can you do which, if you get it right, people will notice with pleasure?

Set out to create a model which others will copy. Get it right first time and your credibility will soar.

SUNDAY

MONDAY

TUESDAY

WEDNESDAY

THURSDAY

FRIDAY

SATURDAY

Fact-check (answers at the back)

1. As Chair, I have the right to:
   a) Expect that people will carry out agreed actions if they have time ❑
   b) Expect that people will carry out agreed actions ❑
   c) Expect that people will carry out agreed actions if they find them sufficiently interesting ❑
   d) Expect that people will carry out agreed actions if, on reflection, they believe that they are appropriate ❑

2. In chairing a meeting:
   a) I believe that anyone attending should already understand the basics of any topic on the agenda ❑
   b) I assume that nobody understands the basics of a topic before we discuss it, so I explain them first ❑
   c) I am not worried about whether or not participants understand a topic before discussion – they will pick it up as they go along ❑
   d) I check that everyone understands the basics of a topic before we discuss it ❑

3. In chairing a meeting, if I do not agree with a participant:
   a) I offer an opposing viewpoint ❑
   b) I have a right to tell them that their viewpoint is wrong ❑
   c) I allow them to have their say anyway ❑
   d) I ask them to be quiet ❑

4. In chairing a meeting:
   a) I allow the most senior people to dominate ❑
   b) I ensure that everyone has an equal opportunity to express their views ❑
   c) I dominate the meeting, because my role is the most important ❑
   d) I make sure that the quietest people get to speak more than the usually vocal people would ❑

5. In chairing a meeting:
   a) I draw out quiet participants where it appears that they can make a useful contribution ❑
   b) I force quiet people to speak so that they don't waste our time by coming to a meeting but contributing nothing ❑
   c) I make no effort to draw out quiet people, because they are making no effort to speak ❑
   d) I prefer that quiet people don't speak because they often embarrass themselves and other participants ❑

6. In chairing a meeting:
   a) I start on time as long as the meeting is quorate ❑
   b) I wait until everyone has arrived before starting ❑
   c) I start on time whether or not we are quorate ❑
   d) I don't pay much attention to timekeeping ❑

7. In chairing a meeting:
a) It doesn't matter whether or not we keep to the agenda ❏
b) It is important that we keep to the agenda ❏
c) It's fine to change the agenda midway if people are not finding the original agenda very interesting ❏
d) I don't usually work from an agenda ❏

8. PMI stands for:
a) Plus, minus, interesting ❏
b) Plus, minus, inconsequential ❏
c) Positive, minus, interesting ❏
d) Plus, minus, inconsistent ❏

9. To resolve conflict:
a) Tell people that you will send them away if they continue to fight ❏
b) Allow them to argue their point and hope that the conflict will burn itself out ❏
c) Toughen up by insisting, for example, that people speak only after raising a hand and that only one person may speak at once ❏
d) Shout at the offending participants ❏

10. It is important that we record:
a) Minutes of the meeting – a verbatim account of the discussions ❏
b) Things which the recorder thought were interesting enough to note ❏
c) Nothing – a record is unimportant ❏
d) Action points – the agreed actions that participants will take after the meeting ❏

THURSDAY

Virtual and other types of meeting

We've focused so far on a fairly traditional style of meeting – bringing people together in small groups to talk to each other face to face. While this remains the most common form of meeting, there are many alternatives.

AND YOU'LL BE ABLE TO TALK TO PEOPLE HUNDREDS OF MILES AWAY.

Increasingly, organizations use technology to cut costs and lower their carbon footprint. It may be considered unethical for participants to travel vast distances when they could as easily talk online or use other technology. Travelling time is expensive and may be unproductive. If you can meet others without leaving the office – indeed, without leaving home – you have a longer day in which to do something useful.

Technology brings its own rewards and challenges, and each form of technology-supported meeting is very different.

A large conference-style meeting has a very different feel to a small group meeting.

Audio meetings are cheap and can be very effective, but don't allow you to see the other participants.

Stand-up meetings – some organizations insist that meeting rooms have no seats!

And let's not forget the humble one-to-one meeting, the mainstay of the appraisal and objective process and one of the most common forms of meeting in working life.

This chapter is all about alternative types of meeting, how they differ from the traditional small group face-to-face meeting and the techniques and skills needed to make them work.

I was once invited from the UK to New York to attend a meeting to discuss a project on which I had been working. I was told that the meeting would last around 45 minutes. As much as I love New York, it would effectively take three working days – travel to New York, attend the meeting, wait for the return flight, fly overnight and return in the early hours of the morning too tired to work effectively.

I asked if the organization had a video conferencing kit. They said they did and I told them that I had it within view of where I was sitting.

They still insisted that I went to see them in person. I asked why and they said 'Because we need a warm body!'.

Audio conferences

Psychology professor Albert Mehrabian has stated that, in face-to-face communication, we only have three ways to communicate – words, voice and non-verbal communication (body language) – and each affects the extent to which we are liked by others: words: 7 per cent; voice: 38 per cent; non-verbal communication: 55 per cent. In audio conferences we lose the ability to see each other and thus the dynamics change. Because we cannot pick up on others' body language, we have to rely more on tone and word choices to create an impression of each other. Some keys to effective participation are to use rich language, modulate your voice, speak as fluently and clearly as you can and listen!

Audio conferences, which require people to dial into a central number and type in a PIN on their telephone, are:

- relatively cheap (compared with face-to-face meetings)
- quick to set up (many organizations have an account with a telecoms company which offers an audio conference service)
- effective for relatively small groups (I once trained 40 people via audio conference, but for a meeting a group of seven to eight people is fine).

We'll assume here that you have called the meeting. To set up an audio conference, call the telecoms service provider to ask for the dial-in number, a PIN code for you as the facilitator and a separate PIN code for the participants. The meeting will typically be shorter than a face-to-face meeting, because people have a lower threshold of concentration when they have only one channel of communication. Your agenda, however, will look very much like the standard agenda which we have already seen. E-mail the agenda and invitation in good time for people to plan to attend, and request confirmations of attendance.

Make sure that you dial in first – ideally a couple of minutes before the meeting starts. It's annoying for participants to be invited to a meeting only to discover that the Chair is not there. As with a face-to-face meeting, start on time to show that you mean business.

It's quite tricky to chair a meeting when you cannot see people. Participants in audio conferences are often side-tracked by e-mails and other distractions, and you need to keep the meeting sharp and snappy and involve participants by name. The audio conference is no place for long speeches.

Take a roll call to check who is on the line (some audio conference facilities announce the names of each person as they join), thank people for attending and state the purpose of the meeting. Reiterate the duration of the meeting, and stay within that time.

You may want to distribute a set of slides or other supporting materials to participants and refer to these during the meeting. This tends to increase engagement, because it gives participants something to look at and something to do with their hands – all of which reduce the likelihood of them losing focus.

Video conferences

Top tips for video conferences:

Test the equipment at each end before the participants arrive – arrange with a colleague in the other location to arrive early and check that the picture and sound are working.

Position chairs so that everyone can be seen. Sit in each seat in turn and ask your colleague to do the same in the other location.

Check that each can see the other in every position and note whether some people will be obscured by others.

Test the sound from different parts of the room. Most video conferencing kits use a flat, circular table-top microphone which should be able to pick up sound from all corners of the room.

Choose a well-lit, well-ventilated room. If you can switch off air conditioning, this will reduce the background noise picked up by the microphone.

Have a facilitator in each location. Their job is to marshal conversation and ensure that only one person at a time is speaking.

Have everyone introduce themselves, location by location.

Ask people to remain relatively still unless they are taking deliberate actions which they intend others to see. Too much movement may become distorted on screen.

Keep the meeting relatively short – an hour is probably long enough.

Ensure that you have the number of the technical support department on hand.

Web meetings

Web meetings are growing in popularity. Broadband internet costs are lower than ever, bandwidth has increased and most working people have internet access at home as well as in the workplace. There are many commercial platforms for web meetings, such as Sametime, Webex and LiveMeeting, which offer a similar set of tools, including desktop sharing, video, a virtual whiteboard, question and answer features, the ability to raise a virtual hand to alert the facilitator, breakout facilities and online chat.

Some organizations find that sound and video drain their internet resources and prefer that only the facilitator (or Chair) be visible through video and that participants speak to each other through standard audio conferencing.

Because you will typically see only the facilitator and not the other participants, you have to be self-disciplined in a web meeting, using the hand-raise tool to tell the facilitator when you want to speak rather than simply talking. If you are using the in-built sound tools, most web-meeting software allows the facilitator to mute everyone and then virtually hand the microphone to participants one at a time.

A big problem with web meetings is that participants, because they cannot see each other, tend to mentally drift off and do other things while the meeting is taking place. Some software shows the facilitator when a participant is doing something else on their computer, and a good facilitator will use the chat facility to send a private message to the offending participant to nudge them back into the meeting. Many facilitators will use the display capabilities to show slides or other visuals to try to engage the participants.

Some golden rules for web meetings:

1 Keep web meetings short – shorter than a face-to-face meeting.
2 Allow a little small talk at the beginning, as you would in a traditional meeting.
3 Set out a clear purpose for the meeting at the outset.
4 Do things in ten-minute bursts with breakouts and variety of presentation to constantly re-engage participants.
5 Make the meetings as interactive as possible – ask opinions, stimulate debate and use the survey/question tool to pose questions.
6 Use video if your infrastructure will stand it.
7 Treat web meetings as seriously as you would any other meeting.

Stand-up meetings (no seats allowed...)

A big complaint about meetings is that they take too long. A simple solution is to remove the seats! The average stand-up meeting takes around 20 minutes, which seems to be the longest that anyone can comfortably stand. Often a high bar-style round table is used for paperwork and to give people a writing surface. Sometimes, participants simply stand.

The benefits:

- speed
- people stick to the point
- decisions are made quickly.

The disadvantages:

- decisions may be made too quickly with insufficient debate
- people become aggressive when others wander away from the point
- some constantly complain that they do not like standing up.

Do not dismiss stand-up meetings before first trying them. In some organizations, they have become the norm.

One of my clients held all of its meetings standing up. They had other rules, too:

Agendas must be posted out at least three days before a meeting.

A maximum of two items could appear on the agenda.

A meeting must last no more than 20 minutes.

Topic owners have 2–3 minutes to speak on their topic and 2–3 minutes' discussion time afterwards.

Action points are recorded and must be e-mailed to participants within 20 minutes of the end of the meeting.

They were (and remain) a remarkably efficient and profitable organization.

Large conference-style meetings

The sheer scale of conference-style meetings demands a level of project management that is unnecessary in a straightforward round-the-table meeting. We'll assume for these purposes that you have been asked to attend one, either as a delegate or as a speaker.

Let's focus here on a few highlights for you as a speaker:

Equipment

● Rather than operate any equipment yourself, you may need a sound technician. The best technicians set sound levels, adjust them a little when participants arrive (because acoustics are different in empty and full rooms) and then leave them alone. They are on hand constantly to monitor and fix any problems as they arise and are otherwise unobtrusive. The worst technicians are obsessive knob-twiddlers, never content with the sound balance and playing with it incessantly to the detriment of the event.

● If you are speaking at the event, check all the equipment before you start.

   – Check whether you will have a collar (lapel) microphone, a microphone taped to your face, a handheld 'lollipop' mike or a fixed mike on a stand or behind a podium. The style of microphone affects your performance. If you are nervous at speaking in front of a large group, go for the lapel mike so you can move around and rid yourself of excess adrenaline, or the lollipop, which allows movement and gives you something to do with your hands, but note that juggling the lollipop and your speaker notes can be tricky!

   – If you are using slides, check how to change them. Some technicians give you a signalling device to tell them when to change or blank a slide. Some give you a remote control allowing you to change the slides yourself. If you are using the former, work through the slides with the technician, showing them which are build slides, for which a single click simply makes the next bullet or image appear. Be aware of sleepy and distracted technicians who miss your signals. If using the remote device, note that you can point it towards the audience and it will still work, rather than pointing at the screen, which means that you have your back to the audience.

Now let's assume that you are a delegate.

Speaking from the floor

If you speak from the floor at a large event, you need to be heard. Usually, someone will hand you a lollipop-style hand-held microphone. You may have witnessed people tapping the end, blowing into them and shouting '1–2–3, testing', which makes them look amateurish. At a well-organized event, the microphone is switched on, the sound level has been checked and the technician has adjusted the volume for the mike you are holding. Most hand-held mikes are directional, so hold them angled just a little down, so people can still see your face as you talk, rather than underneath your chin.

Do not shout – the mike will pick up a normal speaking voice. Speak a little slower than usual because microphones tend to pick up the lower voice tones, and if you speak quickly they have the effect of making you sound as though you are mumbling. Do not gesticulate with your mike hand, because it will move the mike away from your mouth and nobody will be able to hear you.

Ideally, stand up to talk so that people can see you. If you choose not to, for the first few moments after you begin to talk the other participants will be looking around trying to see where your voice is coming from and may miss the first things you say. Be inclusive as you speak, looking around the room and making eye contact with as many people as possible. Be concise, sit down and hand the mike back to whoever gave it to you. Do not switch it off!

Managing a large group

If you are chairing a large meeting, be aware that some people will be nervous at speaking to a large group. It's useful to ask questions of the whole group which demand a show of hands or give participants a red and green card and ask them to show approval or disapproval of an idea by raising their card.

Arrange lots of table group breakout activities. Give table groups flipchart paper and ask them to brainstorm and present back their ideas. Set up competitions between table groups. Introduce variety and interactivity to stimulate the participants and make them feel actively involved.

One-to-one meetings

One-to-one meetings are, by their nature, very personal. When you are arranging a one-to-one meeting, consider the following:

- What is its purpose?
  - For example, appraisal, objective setting, disciplinary, personal development planning, counselling, coaching, mentoring.
- What is the most appropriate location?
  - People feel more comfortable on home ground, so it's a nice concession to go to them rather than have them come to you. Alternatively, you may choose to meet on neutral ground, even out of the workplace.
- How sensitive is the issue?
- How much does the other person need to know in order to prepare for the meeting?
- Stick to the timing you have agreed and do not cancel.
  - This is really important if you are dealing with a sensitive issue. Last-minute cancellation or re-arrangement can be very upsetting for someone who has steeled themselves to come to the meeting.

Partial attendance meetings

Have you ever agreed to attend a meeting because there was one significant agenda item and then found yourself dutifully sitting through irrelevant items, trying not to look bored and desperately wishing you could be somewhere else? People who have no particular vested interest in a subject can bring a fresh perspective to a discussion. Most of us, however, are distracted by the thought of the work piling up in our absences and do not consider these meetings a great use of our time.

If all the invited participants are based in the meeting location, then partial attendance is a useful way to manage your own and others' time. Time slots are allocated to each agenda item and the Chair ensures that the group adheres strictly to those times. A five-minute 'turnaround' break is scheduled between agenda items. During the short break, participants for whom the next topic is irrelevant leave and are replaced by others for whom it is relevant. It's a good way to ensure that the meeting is focused and that the best people are there for each discussion.

There is a danger that if the timings are not accurate then either the core group in the meeting finds it has a lot of spare time on its hands because an item finishes early and the next participants are not yet due, or there is a domino effect on waiting participants if an item overruns from which it may be difficult to recover. Partial attendance meetings rely on good planning and strong chairing.

Summary

Think carefully about the purpose of a meeting, the available budgets and equipment, the locations of the intended participants and the time needed for the meeting, and choose the meeting type accordingly.

This table may help you to decide, assuming that you have access to the relevant equipment. One-to-one meetings are exceptional and have been excluded.

	Traditional face-to-face and partial attendance meetings	Stand-up	Web	Audio	Video	Large conference style
Large number of topics	Y	N	N	N	N	Y
Small number of topics	Y	Y	Y	Y	Y	N
Long meeting	Y	N	N	N	N	Y
Small number of participants	Y	Y	Y	Y	Y	N
Large number of participants	N	N	Y	Y	Y	Y
Low budget	N	Y	Y	Y	Y	N

We have assumed here that stand-up meetings take place between people in the same location (it could be considered rude to invite people to travel some distance to a meeting and then not offer them a seat). You'll notice that web, audio and video all follow the same patterns – low budget, able to accommodate both small and large numbers of participants, and useful when there is a small number of topics and the meeting is designed to be relatively short.

In an organization steeped in tradition, it may be difficult at first to persuade people to break away from the standard face-to-face meeting. Use cost–benefit analysis to persuade people to try other forms of meeting and to use technology. And good luck with the stand-up meetings!

Fact-check (answers at the back)

1. We should consider using technology as an alternative to traditional meetings because:
a) The technology is there, so we may as well use it ☐
b) It may cut costs and lower carbon footprints ☐
c) It's a bit of a novelty ☐
d) It's more fun than a real meeting ☐

2. Albert Mehrabian says that in face-to-face conversation, likeability is based on:
a) Words: 38 per cent, voice: 7 per cent and non-verbal communication: 55 per cent ☐
b) Words: 55 per cent, voice: 38 per cent and non-verbal communication: 7 per cent ☐
c) Words: 7 per cent, voice: 38 per cent and non-verbal communication: 55 per cent ☐
d) Words: 10 per cent, voice: 10 per cent and non-verbal communication: 80 per cent ☐

3. In running an audio conference, I can engage participants by:
a) Distributing slides or other supporting materials for use during the meeting ☐
b) Cracking jokes to amuse them ☐
c) Presenting to them and inviting questions afterwards ☐
d) Asking them to tell funny stories ☐

4. In running a video conference:
a) It's best to have no facilitator ☐
b) It's best to have just one facilitator ☐
c) It's best to rotate the faciliation of the conference ☐
d) It's best to have a facilitator in each location ☐

5. In running a web meeting:
a) The facilitator should leave all microphones on so people can contribute when they wish ☐
b) The facilitator should mute all microphones and hand the virtual microphone to someone who has raised their hand ☐
c) The facilitator should mute all microphones except those belonging to people who can make a real contribution to the meeting ☐
d) The faciliator should not allow anyone else but him/herself to speak ☐

6. Stand-up meetings:
a) Are useful when there are a lot of topics to discuss ☐
b) Are designed to punish unruly participants ☐
c) Are never useful ☐
d) Keep the participants sharply focused ☐

7. In large conference-style meetings:
a) It's best to sit down when speaking from the floor ❏
b) It's best to stand up when speaking from the floor ❏
c) It's best not to contribute from the floor ❏
d) It's best to walk to the front before contributing ❏

8. In a one-to-one meeting:
a) The location is unimportant ❏
b) The location is very important ❏
c) The location is not relevant ❏
d) The location is the most important consideration ❏

9. Partial attendance meetings:
a) Ensure that people only spend time in the sections of the meeting which are relevant to them ❏
b) Effectively put people's expertise on trial ❏
c) Ensure that people do not interfere in areas which do not concern them ❏
d) Have no purpose at all ❏

10. It's important to use alternative types of meeting because:
a) Kids these days are used to technology and so expect to use it for meetings when they first start working ❏
b) Traditional meetings have been shown repeatedly to be useless ❏
c) They may be a better match for the group, the meeting type and the budget ❏
d) We should always try new things ❏

SUNDAY

MONDAY

TUESDAY

WEDNESDAY

THURSDAY

FRIDAY

SATURDAY

FRIDAY

After the meeting

Purposeful meetings are an integral part of a working process. Just as a meeting must be well prepared, so it should be followed up effectively and quickly to ensure that people have completed delegated action points, are working in the ways they agreed during the meeting, are prepared for the next meeting and are happy with the way that the meeting was conducted.

Think of it a little like training. If a group of people attend a training course and afterwards return to their workplace and assume the same old routines, then the training course serves little purpose. If the training is part of a broader programme and the learning from the training is immediately applied in the workplace, then both individuals and the organization will see some benefit from it. If a meeting is seen as an interruption to work and when people return to the workplace nothing changes, then the meeting has served no purpose. Action-based meetings and good follow-up prove the worth of the meeting.

Today we'll look at the things you should do after a meeting, either as a participant or as the Chair of the meeting.

The first follow-up action, a debrief, may actually be taken at the end of the meeting.

Meeting debrief

The most successful organizations are constantly looking for ways to improve. Meeting debriefs are one such method of improvement.

At the end of a meeting, it is useful to discover:

● what worked well and should be continued, either as it stands or with some tweaking
● what could be changed, and how to make future meetings better.

Normally, the Chair leads this discussion. If that's you, you must be sufficiently resilient to take implied or direct criticism. If the meeting didn't work well, some of the reasons may be attributable to you. We looked earlier at single-loop and double-loop learning. The meeting debrief should be an example of double-loop learning, in which we look at the underlying causes of a problem and change our methods so that we do not see the problem again.

Here's some typical feedback that you may hear in a meeting debrief, along with some responses or suggestions for improvement:

● 'I did not feel that people listened to me.'
    – Be cautious here. It may be that the person was boring or what they said was irrelevant. There may be other factions who disagreed with them. Children often claim that nobody is listening to them when what they mean is that nobody agrees with them. Adults sometimes act like children...
● 'I did not get much of a chance to speak.'
    – Be sure that you give people both an equal opportunity to speak and the same air time. If on reflection you did not do this, accept it quietly and tell people that you will make doubly sure next time that people have equal opportunities to speak.
● 'One or two people seemed to dominate the meeting. The rest of us couldn't get a word in edgeways.'
    – As above.

- 'I do not feel we spent enough time on XYZ, which was an important issue.'
  - Explain that timings were given on the agenda, which was distributed some time before the meeting. If participants believe that timings are inaccurate for future meetings, adjust them accordingly.
- 'We spent too much time talking about XYZ and there were more important issues which did not get sufficient air time.'
  - As above.
- 'The meeting was too long.'
  - Ask for a general view on the ideal length for such a meeting. Go with the majority view.
- 'The meeting was too short.'
  - As above.

Action points

As a meeting participant, you will probably have agreed to take certain actions after the meeting. If you do them while the meeting is still fresh in your mind, it's likely that you will do them with more enthusiasm than if you leave them for later. Have you been to a meeting and felt fired up by the discussions and keen to follow up on your agreed actions, but then you go to a different meeting, with a new cast of characters, and suddenly the newer actions you've agreed to undertake seem more interesting?

If we do not act while the memory of a meeting is still fresh, there's a danger we will not complete the actions we committed to at all. When you accept a meeting invitation, schedule time in your diary for the next day to do the follow-up work. Do it immediately and you will associate it with the meeting, and next time you meet the same group it will be easier to remember the actions you took in relation to that meeting.

As the Chair, your responsibilities include distributing action points and following up on them. Ideally, distribute action points within 24 hours of the meeting, so they are still fresh in everyone's minds.
Check the due dates assigned along with the action points, give people one or two days' leeway, and then call them to ask

them about their progress. Be positive and encouraging but do not tolerate poor excuses for inaction. If someone tells you that they have not yet started, ask them when they will and say you will call them again the day after their revised starting date to see how they are getting on. If they have not begun the next time you call, you need to probe a little deeper.

OK MALCOLM – YOU'VE BEEN DELEGATED. ANY QUESTIONS?

Common reasons why people do not do the actions assigned to them:

1 *They were unclear on what they agreed to, but were embarrassed to say so.* Gently help them to understand, without being patronizing or judgemental, so that they feel able to undertake the agreed action with more confidence. Do not make any reference to their embarrassment at the next meeting; treat their now completed action as you would any other.

2 *They are not competent to take the action.* Do not berate them for agreeing because they may have done so in good faith, believing that they were capable and possibly wanting the experience of doing something which later proved too difficult. Ask them what help they need and put them in touch with others who can help them. With luck, the assistance they receive will help them to be self-sufficient next time.

3 *They have other priorities.* So does everyone else the moment they leave a meeting. At the time of the meeting, everything seems terribly important and possibly urgent. After the meeting, we go back to our everyday work and our routine kicks in again.

4 *They claim not to have time.* Be careful of this one. Claims of being busy are not well tolerated in some organizations. In 1938, C. Northcote Parkinson published *Parkinson's Law*,[6] which states that 'Work expands so as to fill the time available for its completion'. No matter what we have to do and how long we have to do it, it will take the time available for that amount of work. When people claim not to have had the time to complete an action, it may be true or it may be that it was simply not a high priority for them. Ask them if they need help from someone else who attended the meeting or if there are any particular obstacles or concerns which make completion difficult.

5 *Organizational politics.* Someone agrees to an action but then falls foul of organizational politics, discovering that the action will arouse political or other sensitivities. You may not be close enough to the politics (nor inclined to get involved) to be able to deal with it. Just try to understand the situation, offer support or encouragement in any way which seems appropriate and hope that the situation can be resolved.

Follow up with people you met for the first time at the meeting

Sometimes you will go to a meeting and meet someone you find inspiring, funny or useful and you'll want to stay in touch with them. You've exchanged business cards or contact details. Now what?

Every contact could some day be useful. You never know when:

● you will need someone else's specialist knowledge
● you will find yourself in a strange town and realize you actually know someone there
● you will want a new job.

It used to be said that six degrees separate any two human beings: we can connect ourselves to anyone else through our own connections, their connections and their connections' connections, etc. The internet-savvy world may have reduced the number to four or five degrees of separation. Even if the person you have just met does not appear to be useful to your career progression now, they may be in future or they may have a network which could be helpful to you.

After a meeting, send a short e-mail to your new contact telling them that it was nice to meet them and commenting on something interesting they said at the meeting. Ask if they would mind you contacting them when you are next in their area. If they agree, do it sooner rather than later to keep the relationship warm. Many people are sloppy e-mail housekeepers and once you have sent them an e-mail, it's likely to remain in their account for a long time. An e-mail is a cheap way to get your name in front of them!

Alternatively, send them an invitation to connect through one of the online business networking services like Plaxo, Ecademy or LinkedIn. The default invitation is not enough – personalize the invitation and follow up when they accept.

If they look really interesting, send them an invitation to a work-related event which you think they may find interesting.

Private resolution of public conflict

Sometimes meetings degenerate into verbal fights. Two opposing parties start to snipe at each other and before long are engaged in a full-blown argument. As Chair, you have a duty to stop the fight. We looked at how you might do this on Wednesday. The danger is that next time the two meet, the fight will resume. Have a quiet conversation with each of them after the meeting to see what the underlying causes of the conflict are and find some way to resolve them.

If emotions are running high at the end of the meeting, it may be difficult to have a rational conversation with either person, so wait a few days before making contact.

Talk to them individually (e-mail is too impersonal). Say that you had observed the friction between them and ask if it was purely related to the discussion topic or whether there is more to it. If the topic inflamed their passions, check that they are happy with the outcome. If it was the person, indicate (gently) that it's important to keep meetings as objective as possible and ask them to try and depersonalize any future arguments.

Preparing the agenda for the next meeting

If you have checked on completed action points, nudged defaulters, talked sagely to those who came close to blows and evaluated the meeting (either at the end or as a separate exercise), then you are in prime position to prepare for the next meeting.

You may want to include:

● a short section on the evaluation of the meeting
● a section on actions taken since the last meeting.

This nicely creates a sense of continuity from one meeting to the next.

Summary

After a meeting, reflect on:

● what you discussed and the impact and importance of the discussions for you, your colleagues and your area of work

● the actions that you have agreed to take and the ways in which you will tackle them

● whether or not the meeting:

– met your personal objectives

– met its overall objectives.

● how the meeting was conducted:

– what you can learn from that, as either participant or Chair

– what you would do differently in future meetings

– who you met and wish to maintain contact with and how you will do so.

● who appears to have personality clashes:

– are you able to do something about it?

Now plan your actions. If you were well organized, you would have allocated time for your action points the day after the meeting.

SUNDAY MONDAY TUESDAY WEDNESDAY THURSDAY FRIDAY SATURDAY

If you were not, now is the time to do this. Schedule time in your diary for the day after your next meeting for follow-up activities. Now prioritize your actions. Tackle the urgent and important ones first, then the important but not urgent ones. If they are neither urgent nor important, there was probably little point in agreeing to them, because nobody will notice whether you do them or not!

Fact-check (answers at the back)

1. It's useful to schedule time in your diary for the day after an important meeting so that:
   a) You can put off going back to your day job ☐
   b) You can take time off because the meeting was exhausting ☐
   c) You can call round the other participants and ask them what they thought of the meeting ☐
   d) You can undertake the actions to which you agreed ☐

2. A meeting debrief is designed to:
   a) Focus on things that went wrong so they can be fixed ☐
   b) Assess what worked well and what can be done better ☐
   c) Focus on things that went well so they can be done again ☐
   d) Assess who was a nuisance so they can be blamed or disciplined ☐

3. If someone claims that they did not have a chance to speak in a meeting, as the Chair you should:
   a) Dismiss the statement as nonsense ☐
   b) Consider whether this was, in fact, the case ☐
   c) Tell them they should speak up a bit ☐
   d) Not invite them to future meetings ☐

4. If someone claims that too much time was given to a single agenda item at the expense of the others:
   a) Dismiss the statement as nonsense ☐
   b) Tell them that they can have their turn to speak on a favourite topic at the next meeting ☐
   c) Explain that the timings appeared on the agenda which was circulated before the meeting ☐
   d) Tell them that you are in charge of timing but they have the right to question it ☐

5. It's best to take action immediately after a meeting because:
   a) It gets it out of the way so we can get back to our everyday work ☐
   b) We work better when the issues are fresh in our mind ☐
   c) It will keep the Chair happy, which is what it's all about ☐
   d) It's generally more interesting than our real work ☐

6. A common reason why people do not undertake their assigned actions is:
   a) They never intended to take the actions ☐
   b) They agreed to the action to appear to be doing something useful ☐
   c) They were not clear on the action, but embarrassed to admit it ☐
   d) They are too lazy ☐

SUNDAY MONDAY TUESDAY WEDNESDAY THURSDAY FRIDAY SATURDAY

7. In following up with new contacts after a meeting:
a) It's useful to send a personalized invitation to connect through an online networking service ❏
b) It's useful to send the default invitation to connect through an online networking service, because you do not want to appear overfamiliar ❏
c) It's best to wait for them to contact you ❏
d) It's useful to wait a few weeks to test whether or not they still remember you ❏

8. If two people argue fiercely during a meeting:
a) It's best to berate them publicly during the meeting ❏
b) It's best to talk to them individually a few days after the meeting ❏
c) It's best never to mention it again ❏
d) It's best to talk to them together a few days after the meeting ❏

9. In preparing the agenda for the next meeting:
a) It's useful to include items which suggest continuity between meetings ❏
b) It's best to avoid apparent continuity so that the approach is completely fresh each time ❏
c) It doesn't matter whether or not there is any sense of continuity between meetings ❏
d) It's useful to reverse the order of the last agenda to keep participants on their toes ❏

10. Parkinson's law states:
a) 'Work contracts so as to fill the time available for its completion' ❏
b) 'Work contracts so as to allow it to be completed within the allotted time' ❏
c) 'Work expands so as to fill the time available for its completion' ❏
d) 'Work expands so as to take more time than is available for its completion' ❏

SATURDAY

The perfect meeting

Today we'll bring together everything you have learned this week in the form of a short story.

We'll meet two fairly junior members of an organization who have been asked to set up and run an important in-house meeting. Although they have attended many meetings, they have no experience of running one themselves. We'll see through their mistakes and the solutions they find how to set up, run and follow up after the perfect meeting. Along the way, they note what they would do differently next time. You may find their notes helpful in planning and running your own perfect meetings.

Meet the characters

Bob and Pat are junior managers in a large service industry. Each had an internship with the company the summer before their final year at university, and they started together at the company three years ago on a graduate induction programme. They are bright, ambitious and always seeking development opportunities. Bob is cautious and concerned about what others think about him. Pat throws caution to the wind and sometimes takes actions without considering the consequences. She is often frustrated by Bob's conservatism. He is scared that she will do something which casts them both in a bad light. Despite this, they are close colleagues, often working together, and they socialize with the same group outside work.

An instruction from above

Their director, Alison, sees running a meeting as a relatively high-profile development opportunity for them. She has given them an outline of the purpose of the meeting, a list of participants to be invited and told them that, because she is tied up in a project over the next couple of weeks, they should do everything they can to arrange the meeting, one of them should chair it and they should talk to her only if they encounter any issues which they cannot resolve.

Determining the purpose

Bob and Pat study the outline for the meeting.

'It's a bit vague, isn't it?', says Bob. 'It says it's a meeting of the regional directors to plan staff training and development and associated budgets over the next two years.'

'Seems clear enough to me', says Pat. 'What more do you need?'

Bob is unhappy at the lack of detail. He doesn't know many directors, knows little about current staff training and development plans, and doesn't know where to start with the agenda.

Pat scans the list of participants and sees that the HR Director, who is responsible for staff development, will be attending the meeting. She picks up the phone to call him. Bob stops her, saying that they should first decide what they need to know to get the best from the call. Between them they agree that they should find out about:

1 current training and development plans
2 significant planned and expected events in the organization which may have an effect on training and development
3 current training development budgets
4 attitudes of the directors towards training and development.

Pat makes the call. The HR Director, although pleasant, is busy. He offers to e-mail them the current plans and budget details but says that he is not in the best position to talk about planned and expected events. They should speak to someone else about this – he is vague about who could help them. He feels he would be speaking out of turn if he commented on other directors' attitudes, and this is something best gauged during the meeting. Bob is concerned that he sounds offended at the question. Pat is unconcerned.

They debate whether or not to call Alison and decide not to bother her just yet. They think they have enough to start creating an agenda. Pat makes a mental note:

> **Always determine the purpose of a meeting and discover as much as you can about it before attending**

Setting the agenda

Bob has checked back through the files and discovered that the regional directors usually use a standard agenda for their meetings. He talks to Alison's secretary, who provides a copy and remarks that this agenda is for their quarterly meetings, but that this is an additional, exceptional meeting called before the budgets are finalized because it could result in a big spend. She is unsure whether the standard agenda will work.

The standard agenda says:

● Action points from last meeting
● Director's report: Northern region

- Director's report: Southern region
- Director's report: Midlands region
- Review of action points
- Next steps and date of next meeting

'Doesn't tell us much', says Pat. 'Let's write our own.'

Bob is worried that any deviation from the standard agenda will annoy the directors, but Pat reminds him that this is an extraordinary meeting with a specific purpose and so the standard agenda is not relevant. Bob notes:

> **Create an agenda which is relevant to the purpose of the meeting**

They agree that they should talk through everything they know about the meeting and logically think through what will help them to get to the desired outcome – planning training and development over the next two years and creating a high-level budget for it.

Participants, they decide, will need to know where they stand now and where they anticipate the company is going – the current level of spending on training and development, the current breadth and depth of training and development offered throughout the company, any planned major projects which may generate a training spend and any forecast changes to the business which may in turn create training needs.

'Some of this we can provide as background reading', says Bob. 'We have the current plans and budget details. If people read this in advance they will be better prepared for discussion. I imagine each of the directors, if they are interested in people's development, will come up with ideas of how they would like to develop their own staff, and between them they should have some good ideas about things which may affect the plans and the spend.'

Pat is impressed. She jots a note to herself:

> It doesn't all have to be done in the meeting. Pre-reading can cut down on tedious discussion!

They begin to sketch out an agenda and assign names to specific topics:

Meeting subject: Determine the staff training plans and high-level budgets for the next two years from 1 May

Meeting objectives: Agree on the major requirements for training and development for all staff in the next two-year period, and estimate the costs of the training for budgetary purposes

Meeting organizers: Bob Jenkins and Pat Wilson

Meeting recorder: Vanessa Barton (they assume that Alison's PA will record the meeting)

Names of invited participants: Alison Meads, James Law, Selma Goode, Frank Abbott, Delia Mays

Venue, date and time: Meeting Room 14, HQ, 7 April, 09:45 am

Pre-meeting reading: Current year training plans and training budget (attached)

Apologies for absence

09:30	Coffee
09:45	Welcome and purpose
10:00	Review of current training plans and budget (Frank Abbott, HR Director)
10:30	Training requirements for Northern region (Selma Goode, Regional Director North)
10:45	Training requirements for Southern region (James Law, Regional Director South)

11:00	Training requirements for Midlands region (Delia Mays, Regional Director Midlands)
11:15	Anticipated business changes which will create training and development needs (all)
11:45	Proposed high-level budget requirements (all)
12:30	Summary of action points
12:45	Close

Happy that this covers everything, Bob insists that they ask Alison to review it before sending it out. A wise move, because she raises a number of issues in her e-mail back to them:

Bob, Pat

A nice start, but a few changes needed before sending it. Subject and purpose are fine. Best to ask me before commandeering Vanessa for half a day. She's far too busy and I can't spare her. While one of you is chairing, the other could record the meeting.

You've left the Ops Director, Bill Jones, off the list. He'll be mad if he doesn't get an invite and he always has something to contribute. If we start at 09:30, those travelling some way will have to come down the night before. You'll need to book hotels for them. Don't have the meeting in-house – you'll never get them to stay in the meeting room for two consecutive minutes. Take it offsite and don't spend more than the agreed limits. You're expecting people to have the bladder of a camel – no break for nearly four hours? I don't think so! You'll need to stretch the session on budgets a bit – always leads to an argument, so lunch will be needed. Could you please revamp it – I don't need to see it again before you send it.

Alison

The pair revise the agenda:

09:30	Coffee
09:45	Welcome and purpose
10:00	Review of current training plans and budget (Frank Abbott, HR Director)
10:30	Training requirements for Northern region (Selma Goode, Regional Director North)
10:45	Training requirements for Southern region (James Law, Regional Director South)

11:00	Break
11:15	Training requirements for Midlands region (Delia Mays, Regional Director Midlands)
11:30	Anticipated business changes which will create training and development needs (all)
12:00	Proposed high-level budget requirements (all)
13:00	Summary of action points
13:15	Close

The venue

Bob and Pat are uneasy about choosing an offsite venue and remember that the training manager, Jean Philips, uses a number of outside locations for training. She recommends a local hotel which provides sizeable meeting rooms and a good service at a reasonable delegate rate. They call, ascertain that a room is free on their required date and book it.

Preparing for the meeting

Pat sends out the agendas with an e-mail cover note and the background reading attached. Its subject is 'Training meeting' and the body of the note simply says 'Meeting agenda attached. Please respond asap.'

A week before the event, Pat has heard from nobody and Bob suggests they call each participant to check that they are coming. They are surprised when several directors deny receiving anything and, on searching for the e-mail, find it and say they had no idea what it was about so filed it for later reading. Some are angry because they had made other plans for the meeting day. They ask where the meeting is taking place and what it's about. Pat is tempted to tell them that all the detail is in the attachment, but holds back, sensing that they are already sufficiently annoyed. Ultimately, all agree to come.

Pat jots another note to herself:

> Next time I send out an agenda, spell out in the cover note what it's about, when it is and who people should respond to

Bob calls the hotel to finalize the arrangements. He has arranged the catering, asked that the room be set up in boardroom style, and requested a flipchart, pens, and a projector and screen. He has also arranged for those staying overnight before the meeting to stay at the same venue. He intends to provide his own laptop for the directors to show their slides.

The day of the meeting

Bob and Pat arrive an hour and a half before the meeting is due to start. Immediately, they encounter problems:

- The room is difficult to find and badly signposted.
- The power cable from the projector is trailing dangerously across the floor to the wall socket.
- The venue has provided whiteboard markers instead of flipchart markers.
- There is almost no space between and behind chairs.
- The room is small and claustrophobic and the air conditioning is noisy.

Bob talks to the conference administrator who, although happy to move the group to another room, says that the only other available room is a good deal bigger and there will be an additional charge for it. They have no flipchart markers ('Nobody ever complained before') and they promise to put up signs and tape down the cables. By 08:30, they have moved to a lighter, airier room with more space and good ventilation.

At 08:30 Alison arrives, a little flustered: 'I arrived at reception and nobody know who I was. When I told them which meeting I was coming to they directed me to the room number you gave on the agenda but there was nobody there. It's taken me five minutes to find you here.'

Pat explains that they have moved and the reasons why, and rushes to reception to tell them who's coming and where to direct people. Finally, the administrator puts up signs directing the participants to the appropriate room.

Alison asks where the agendas and other paperwork are. Bob says that he assumed people would bring it with them. Alison laughs and tells him to go and make copies.

Bob makes a mental note:

> Be explicit about what you need in the meeting room.
>
> Check out the room and equipment before the day of the meeting.
>
> Make additional copies of any required paperwork before the meeting begins.
>
> Ensure that receptionists know who to expect and where to send them.

Participants start to arrive, but by 09:45 two who are driving to the meeting from out of the area are still missing. Pat is keen that the meeting start, but Alison tells her that for this particular meeting they need everyone there from the beginning. Finally, at 10:00, the two other directors arrive. They say that they spent 15 minutes circling, trying to find parking and, unfamiliar with the area, had to spend another 15 minutes walking from the car park to the venue.

Pat makes another note:

> Always send out a map, directions and details of nearby parking.

Alison tells them to start. Pat is chairing and Bob is recording. The meeting starts well, and everyone is engaged and interested. Before James begins his report he asks Pat where his slides are. Bewildered, she says she hasn't got them. James insists that his secretary e-mailed them this morning. She explains that she came straight from home to the venue and didn't know that she should have expected the slides. James is annoyed but has the good grace to realize that she was not told in advance to expect the slides. Bob asks if he has them on a USB memory stick – luckily he does, and Bob sets them up for him quickly and the moment passes.

Bob and Pat both make a mental note:

> Ask for supporting materials before the event.

Everything continues smoothly until the discussion of expected business changes. Bill Jones mentions that one of the best call centre team leaders is leaving and Frank is furious, asking why he hadn't been told. Before long, they are having a full-blown row and Pat does not know what to do. Finally, she calls out 'Gentlemen, it's important that we stick to the agenda. Could you please continue this discussion after the meeting? For now, we need to continue our discussions. Could I ask you please to remain objective in your discussions, rather than letting them become personal.' Bill and Frank hang their heads like naughty schoolchildren and out of the corner of her eye Pat sees Alison give her an almost imperceptible wink. The rest of the meeting is uneventful.

At the end, Bob reads back the action points. Because Bob is so fastidious that they are an accurate and uncontested record of what was agreed.

Lunch

The sandwich lunch has arrived and participants seem to be tucking in happily. All except Delia, who asks where the vegetarian sandwiches are. Bob says he wasn't aware that she had requested any and Delia says she assumed that any self-respecting venue would provide them without being asked. Bob says he will see what he can do and, on discovering that it will take at least 30 minutes for the venue's caterers to produce anything else, hurries to a local shop, where he buys a selection of vegetarian sandwiches, borrows a plate from a sandwich trolley outside a neighbouring meeting room and brings in the sandwiches. Delia appears very happy with them.

After the meeting

Bob and Pat meet Alison on the afternoon of the meeting to discuss what happened and what they learnt. Above all, they say, it's about attention to detail – walking through every stage as though you are a delegate, anticipating problems and not making assumptions. Alison tells them that, all in all, they have done a good job for a first attempt and that the other directors commented on how well the meeting ran.

'Now', says Alison, 'who's going to chase up the actions, and who's going to bang Bill and Frank's silly heads together?'

Summary

In the end the meeting was a success.

There were no major disasters and things which could have gone wrong were spotted early and remedial action was taken. Bob and Pat learnt a good deal from their experience and summarized well what they would do next time – walk through each element from the participants' point of view and avoid making assumptions.

Let's look at the truth behind those assumptions:

The assumption	The truth
People will read the invitation to a meeting	Only if it's absolutely clear that they are being invited to something. Be absolutely explicit
Unbidden, participants will send you slides and other supporting materials before the meeting	No they will not. You will need to ask for them
Participants will bring agendas and other supporting materials with them	Some will and some will not. Print additional copies for the defaulters
They will find the venue without difficulty	No they will not! Unless you send explicit directions, someone will struggle to find it
They will find a parking space	No they will not. Send them a map showing the local parking, the venue and the distance between the two
They will find their way from the car park to the venue	No they will not. Send them a map and directions from one to the other
Meeting rooms will meet high health and safety standards	They will not, because they are not designed by a Health and Safety Officer. Inspect the room for possible hazards before a meeting
Venues will automatically cater for special dietary requirements	Sometimes they will. Often they will not. Tell them in advance exactly what you want
Signage at meeting venues is generally good	It can vary enormously from completely absent to very detailed
Receptionists will know that your meeting is taking place, the correct room number and the names of people who will be attending	Only if you tell them. Take a list of participants to a venue and give it to the receptionist along with your mobile number to call if there are any problems

Fact-check (answers at the back)

1. Immediately after Alison's briefing, Bob and Pat:
   a) Had sufficient information to create the agenda ❑
   b) Had insufficient information to create the agenda ❑
   c) Had insufficient information to create a good agenda, but it didn't matter ❑
   d) Had far too much information to create the agenda, which just proved confusing ❑

2. The biggest problems which Bob and Pat faced arose because:
   a) What can go wrong will go wrong ❑
   b) The directors deliberately made things difficult for them ❑
   c) They lacked the experience to do anything properly ❑
   d) They made assumptions and did not walk through the plans step by step ❑

3. Was Pat correct in saying that much of the information about plans and budgets could be sent out as pre-reading?
   a) No, because the information should be read out during the meeting ❑
   b) No, because nobody would read it ❑
   c) Yes – it freed up time in the meeting for informed discussion ❑
   d) Yes, to test whether anyone actually does the pre-reading ❑

4. Were Bob and Pat safe to take a recommendation for a venue without checking it out for themselves?
   a) Yes, they should trust other people ❑
   b) It was risky – they were lucky this time ❑
   c) Yes. A venue is a venue. They are all pretty much the same ❑
   d) Absolutely not – they were very misguided ❑

5. Was it reasonable to assume that the venue would signpost the meeting room without a request to do so from Bob and Pat?
   a) No – it's best to set out precisely what you need ❑
   b) Yes – a venue should do these things automatically ❑
   c) It doesn't matter either way. People should be able to find their way to the meeting room without help ❑
   d) No – they should have made and taken their own signs ❑

6. Should a venue ensure that cables are taped down so that nobody trips over them?
a) No, it should be the responsibility of the meeting organizer ❏
b) No, people should have the sense to notice and step over loose cables ❏
c) Yes they should. Any professional venue should do this as a matter of course, especially when they provided the equipment ❏
d) Yes, and we should be prepared to sue any venue which fails to do so ❏

7. Was it safe for Bob and Pat to assume that people would bring agendas and other paperwork with them?
a) Yes, it's reasonable to assume that people will bring everything they need ❏
b) No – people cannot be relied on to do anything properly ❏
c) Yes. It would be unusual for professional people to forget anything ❏
d) Sadly not. People are forgetful and it's best to accommodate their forgetfulness ❏

8. Should Bob and Pat have sent out maps and directions?
a) Yes – it's a courtesy when people are coming to an unfamiliar area ❏
b) No – people should be able to find their own way ❏
c) They should not have chosen a venue which was hard to find ❏
d) No – they should simply have sent the address and the postcode ❏

9. Was Pat right to handle the dispute in the way she did?
a) Absolutely not. What she said was rude and made it worse because she was junior to the other people in the meeting ❏
b) It's a tricky one – maybe she was, maybe she wasn't ❏
c) Absolutely. In a formal meeting, the Chair outranks everyone else and has the right to be assertive in keeping order and getting the meeting back on track ❏
d) No, because she should not have been allowed to chair the meeting in the first place ❏

10. Is it reasonable to assume that a venue will cater for special dietary requirements without being asked to do so?
a) No, but they should be able to produce something appropriate on the day, whatever the requirements ❏
b) Yes – they should know that people have different dietary needs ❏
c) People should not be so fussy – they should eat what they are given ❏
d) No – it's best to tell them what you want ❏

SUNDAY

MONDAY

TUESDAY

WEDNESDAY

THURSDAY

FRIDAY

SATURDAY

Surviving in tough times

Successful meetings can drive business success. A theme throughout the book is the need to ensure that every meeting has real purpose, and this is never more relevant than in tough economic times. Consider carefully the real priorities of your business, what can be done without first holding a meeting to discuss it and what really would benefit from collective thinking in a meeting. If you invite only those who can make a real contribution on the key issues, start your meetings on time, keep the participants focused, upbeat and purposeful, then it will help you to weather the storm.

1 Adopt a no blame culture

In tough times, it's all too easy to allow tensions to overflow into blame, but blame is a waste of energy which you could channel more usefully into planning positive change. Make your meetings a blame-free environment.

2 Stick to time

When people are under increased pressure to perform, they cherish every spare moment of time. Stick to your meeting timetable – nobody will be upset if a meeting finishes early, but you'll create enmity if you overrun.

3 Chair with confidence and focus

Take charge of the meetings you chair and keep them focused on the agenda by limiting side conversations and encouraging positive contributions.

4 Use positive language in meetings

When people are down or struggling to succeed in difficult times, they thrive on positivity. Without being over-optimistic, talk in positive language about what can be achieved, making no reference to what cannot. You'll be surprised at the impact this has on meeting participants.

5 Revisit your business strategy

One of the best purposes for a meeting in tough times is to revisit your group or business strategy. Strategy is all about direction and scope of work and, when clearly defined and communicated, it can help people to focus on the real priorities, drawing them together with common purpose, rather than allowing them to be too task-focused and to adopt a silo mentality.

6 Use technology in place of face-to-face meetings

When you are under pressure to save money and time, use video, audio or web-based conferencing.

7 Only invite people to relevant sections

People under time pressure cannot afford to spend time sitting through agenda items which are not relevant to them. Invite people to attend only the sections of the meeting that are relevant (possible when the meeting is virtual or in their office location).

8 Reduce the cost of catering

Time meetings so that lunch is unnecessary. Keep them relatively short so that they don't coincide with meal times.

9 Focus on actions

In times of deep recession, people will cling to whatever gives them a sense of control and purpose. Ensure that discussions result in practical, achievable actions to reinforce that sense of purpose and regaining of control.

10 Think how you will communicate the outcomes and actions of your meetings

Include a standard agenda item 'the stories we will tell' at the end of your meetings. Discuss what you will tell people about the outcomes of the meeting and how you will describe them, then ask each participant to go out and tell a number of people what you have discussed. This way you stem rumours and control the rumour mill, which is rife in difficult times, rather than be at the mercy of uninformed rumours.

Answers

Sunday: 1b; 2c; 3a; 4b; 5c; 6d; 7d; 8a; 9c; 10b.

Monday: 1a; 2d; 3a; 4b; 5a; 6d; 7a; 8b; 9d; 10c.

Tuesday: 1c; 2a; 3b; 4d; 5a; 6b; 7d; 8c; 9b; 10a.

Wednesday: 1b; 2d; 3c; 4b; 5a; 6a; 7b; 8a; 9c; 10d.

Thursday: 1b; 2c; 3a; 4d; 5b; 6d; 7b; 8b; 9a; 10c.

Friday: 1d; 2b; 3b; 4c; 5b; 6c; 7a; 8b; 9a; 10c.

Saturday: 1b; 2d; 3c; 4b; 5a; 6c; 7d; 8a; 9c; 10d.

References

1. A Network MCI Conferencing White Paper. Meetings in America: A study of trends, costs and attitudes toward business travel, teleconferencing, and their impact on productivity (Greenwich, CT: INFOCOMM, 1998), 3.

2. Nelson RB and Economy P, *Better Business Meetings* (Burr Ridge, IL: Irwin Inc., 1995), 5.

3. A Network MCI Conferencing White Paper. Meetings in America: A study of trends, costs and attitudes toward business travel, teleconferencing, and their impact on productivity (Greenwich, CT: INFOCOMM, 1998), 10.

4. Tuckman B. 'Developmental sequence in small groups'. *Psychological Bulletin* (1965) 63(6): 384–99.

5. Glasser W. *Choice Theory: A New Psychology of Personal Freedom.* (New York: HarperPerennial, 1999).

6. Northcote Parkinson C. *Parkinson's Law: The Pursuit of Progress.* (London: John Murray, 1958).